Playing in Living Water

Practising a Prayerful Life

Jennifer Goodyer

Be willing to be a beginner every single morning.
-Meister Eckhart

For Henry and Phoebe.

Contents

Foreword

by The Reverend Doctor Leslie Griffiths,
Lord Griffiths of Burry Port

When I finally put this little book down, I found myself scratching my head in wonderment. A curious reversal of roles seemed to have happened. I felt as if it wasn't I who had read the book but that it had read me. That may sound a strange thing to say. Indeed, it is a strange thing to say. So, I must ask you to be patient with me as I try to explain.

I'd been asked to read part of a book on prayer just to offer my opinion on matters of style. Ever happy to oblige, I suggested they send me a chapter which they did. It was entitled "Praying with Our Intellects." It wasn't long and didn't take much time to read. But it was enough. I was hooked. I asked for the whole manuscript and, sure enough, the writing which I'd so admired - pellucid, engaging, accessible, deceptively simple, had sustained those qualities from start to finish. From the point of view of style, this was a winner.

That wasn't all, however. From the outset it presented me with a challenge. I saw that the author had set herself the goal of serving two kinds of reader. The first, "hungry for practices that open up prayer, [might be] focused on experiencing God and nurturing a relationship with God." The other she identified as someone who might be "intrigued by prayer and by spirituality [but somehow] apprehensive." The first would be on an inside track wanting to know more; the other on an outside track either because they hadn't yet found a way to get further in or else because they'd once been on the inside before circumstances, possibly hurtful, drove them out.

Neither of these described my case. So that ought to have been that. I considered myself a "post-prayer" Christian. Over the years I seem to have tried everything. And yet, again and again, after varying amounts of time, I discarded them all. From the beginning of my life as a Christian, I've flirted with methods and models and models and methods of prayer. In my early years it was John Baillie and William Barclay who fed my prayer-life. They'd compiled books of prayers for every day – I turned their pages, recited their beautifully written material, for months and months. Michel Quoist had his uses too for a while. So did a rosary. I fingered the beads, said prayers for joy and for sorrow, muttered the Jesus prayer in an arcane mantra. From there, I graduated to Taizé materials, loved the singing, enjoyed the litanies, did it all in French as well as in English. And then there were the psalms. I dived into them—in Welsh as well as English, in Coverdale's version as well as Gelineau's. Eventually, I graduated to the intricate Offices put together by the Joint Liturgical Group—this had me sticking three fingers in different pages in order to "do" everything in the right order. I spent decades making these experiments. They all ran into the ground. I kept reaching the point where I felt I was just going through the motions, mouthing words, performing a duty. I gave them all up. I came to see that there was an important distinction to be made between "prayer" and "saying prayers." I wanted my whole being to be as near as possible in a "state of prayer" rather than to reduce prayer to a mechanistic exercise. It all had to do with the heightening of awareness—seeing not only a universe in a wild flower but beauty in an ugly life, hope in the midst of despair, light shining through the cracks. And so, I gave up saying prayers and, instead, worked on an agenda that might offer my utmost to God's highest.

That's where I was when I picked up Jennifer Goodyer's manuscript. Indeed, that is where I still am. But, in no time at all, I found that she'd drawn me into the inner working of her mind. Despite myself. Her style is disarmingly simple. But its content is amazingly profound. She found a way through my defences and somehow (I still don't know how) she spoke to my inner being. She seemed to identify with the fact that people can and do get fed up with vain repetitions, meaningless babbling and the heaping up of empty phrases. Yet there wasn't a suspicion of disapproval, no insistence on my trying harder, no reproof. This is not a guilt-inducing book. I found its simple honesty so compelling and its readiness to engage with my anomie so down-to-earth.

She does this by offering a myriad of ways in which the ordinary experiences of everyday life can be explored for their "prayer dimension." It's as if everything around us is heavy with the possibilities of prayer. All we have to do is open ourselves to it, suss it out, let it wash over us, speak to us, enter the fibre of our being. And she fleshes all this out with some amazingly rich modelling exercises. Not all of them will suit everybody. We all bring our different metabolisms and mind-sets to anything we might call reflection.

Prayer, says our author, is "a natural overflow from the deep place in our soul ... [it is] beyond words." We can "sit in silence enjoying God, [we can] let God sing love's song over us." We can "let go of our tendency to judge worth by results," we need not moralize, we can take "the journey from the head to the heart." There will be moments when we experience "dryness in prayer," when it all becomes a wrestling match, when we drive into ourselves in inappropriate ways, when all seems "heaviness". But, alongside those moments, there are times when the doors of prayer swing open, when we enter into our prayers "with joy and spontaneity," when we can go "rummaging for God." All this will engage our creativity, appeal to our sense of humour, lift up our hearts. And, quoting C.S. Lewis, it will evoke a creedal statement of incredible beauty: "I believe in Christianity as I believe that the Sun has risen – not only because I see it but because, by it, I see everything else." We enter these moments through doors of perception and find ourselves alive with the sense of God's presence.

One look at the Table of Contents in this book took my mind to another one—the one that launches the first Methodist Hymn Book published in 1780. The fourth part of that seminal work contains 283 hymns composed for what the Wesley brothers described as "believers." This is the great throbbing heart of what must surely be the finest hymn book of all time. Here are hymns to nurture the faith, hope, and love of those who have entered the portals of belief. They are organised into ten sections. These are hymns for believers who are rejoicing, fighting, praying, watching, working, suffering, groaning for full redemption, brought to the birth, saved, and interceding for the world. They offer a rich panoply that covers every aspect of the life of faith.

Jennifer Goodyer does something similar for prayer. She arranges her material into ten sections. Here are chapters that encourage praying—with scripture, nature, our intellects, our bodies, the story of our lives; with and for others; with our imaginations, our creativity; with technology, and with silence. Once again a rich exploration, this time spread across the spectrum of prayer.

When I add all this up it's clearly far more than a matter of mere arithmetic. It's more about quality than quantity. Here's an author who refuses to let her hints and clues, her offers and suggestions, the exercises and the experiments she puts forward, turn into inflexible modes or methods or techniques. They remain fluid. There is always somewhere else to go. And here's the miracle of it all. For me at least. To my mind she offers much more than help with "saying prayers." Here is material shot through with the colours of being at prayer, of being in a state of prayer, of finding times that are pregnant with prayers awaiting their birth. This is the "Art of Prayer" and I've loved every part of it.

A Note to My Readers

I have written this book with two readers in mind. The first reader is hungry for practices that open up prayer; for practical ways to enter into a more intentional and intimate relationship with God. This reader is my enthusiast, the one who is eager to begin, or begin again, and who is willing to jump in head-first, or at least wade in fairly quickly. The second reader is more cautious. This reader is intrigued by prayer and by spirituality but is also apprehensive. Perhaps they wonder if they are doing it right or enough or whether prayer can really be expansive and playful. Sometimes I imagine that this reader has had some uncomfortable or damaging experiences of religion or spirituality, or that they have fallen out of love with organised religion and now see themselves as spiritual but not religious.

To both these readers I want to say thank you. You have helped to guide this project and have been my companions. I care for you both and hope you will find nourishment in the pages that follow. You do, however, have different needs and it's to meet these needs that I've given the book its structure. To explain, let me address you separately.

To my enthusiastic reader,

I imagine you dipping in and out of this book, trying on the different practices and noticing how those practices feel and whether they seem to refresh or deepen prayer. To help you navigate the variety of practices contained within this book, I have kept the practices distinct and have referenced them separately in the Contents. I hope this will make it easier to locate favourite or intriguing practices and to share them with others.

Beloved reader, I encourage you to go slowly and to take time to reflect on your experience of each of the practices and to view this reflection as something integral to prayer; a way of deepening your experience of prayer. After each new practice, try to spend a few minutes sitting with your experience, freely sharing your honest thoughts and feelings with God, not as a distant someone, somewhere "out there" but a presence already surrounding you and within you at your deepest level. This reflecting might take the form of spoken words, journaling, an inner dialogue or a bodily check-in. The form doesn't matter but allowing space for your experience of prayer to settle is helpful as a way of becoming more familiar with what is life-giving and what is not. Noticing resistance is important and our more uncomfortable experiences can often teach us as much as those that comfort us, although I do hope you will go gently with anything you encounter that feels fragile or raw.

To my cautious reader,

I imagine you as receptive yet guarded and for reasons I can't quite pinpoint; perhaps you can't either. It's for you that I have clustered the practices around ten themes or modes of prayer and have written an introduction to each. I imagine you focusing your attention on the introductions to these sections and perhaps only scanning the practices. I understand that you may still be deciding how you feel about prayer or Christianity or spirituality or about how they connect with you and your own experiences. Please know that there is no rush to come to a decision and no need to make certainty your destination. I encourage you to give yourself the time and space you need to sit with your questions, your hopes and your doubts. It is for you that I have written the reflection questions at the end of each introduction. I hope that you will linger over these and that they may help you to digest the material and receive it as something offered to you.

Beloved reader, may you come to befriend your questions, doubts, hopes, and sadnesses, no longer seeing them as problems to be solved but openings onto a deeper self-awareness and relationship with God who cares tenderly for you, just as you are.

God's love is expansive and includes all. This invitation to be loved by God and awakened to becoming love for others is, for me, the essence of Jesus' good news and what it means to be a Christian.It is from this perspective that I write this book but, even if you feel uneasy with the word "Christian", I hope you will still find something to refresh you here.

Before I close this preliminary note, I want to acknowledge the mysterious third reader who has never taken form in my mind but has ever been at the periphery of my imagination. Beloved reader, you too have guided this work. I have wondered about you: who you might be and what you might need. Because I can't describe you or articulate your motivations or needs, I can't offer you any specific encouragement or advice. I do, however, extend you a very warm welcome. I hope that I have framed what follows in a way that is invitational and open-ended and that there may be something here to nourish you. Blessed be the longing that brought you here; may you find what your heart desires.

Introduction

This book isn't, primarily, a book about prayer or a book of prayers. It's an encouragement to say yes to the invitation to pray as you are in unselfconscious freedom. You don't need to be different. You don't need to be certain about who you are or who God is or what God wants for you. You can bring your hopes, fears, desires, and doubts, even doubts about God. The invitation is simply to come and be yourself. You are free and welcome to speak and listen and weep and laugh. There is no right way. You are welcome to explore and experiment, to play with prayer with the help of the practices contained within these pages.

Perhaps, as you read on, your yes to this invitation will be a loud and confident shout. Perhaps it will be a tentative whisper. Perhaps it will be reverent and silent. Perhaps you will be intrigued but resistant. Perhaps you will find yourself longing to say yes but unable. All these responses and more are welcome. The invitation remains. It is always the same and always for you.

This book's encouragement to say yes to prayer comes via two sections. The first section consists of several reflections on the nature of prayer. These ground the later practices and offer a starting point for those new to prayer, or new to a more expansive understanding of prayer. These pieces are the fruit of honest reflection on my spiritual life and experience of prayer as well as theological study. To reflect this, I have included personal anecdotes as well as some biblical references and theological reflection. My focus, however, is on you, my reader, and I write hoping to assist you in reflecting on, and going deeper into, your own experiences. To invite a slower, more meditative reading, I have divided this section into eight short chapters which connect to each other but can also be read alone. Each of these ends with a question that invites you to notice your response to what is being offered.

The second section is longer and contains many different spiritual practices that invite and open onto prayer. These practices are grouped into ten chapters:

Praying with Scripture
Praying with Nature
Praying with Our Intellects
Praying with Our Bodies
Praying with the Story of Our Lives
Praying with and for Others
Praying with Our Imaginations
Praying with Our Creativity
Praying with Technology
Praying with Silence

Each of these chapters contains an introduction followed by a selection of practices. Every practice begins with a brief explanatory note and a step-by-step guide to practising. This step-by-step guide is not intended to be prescriptive but is offered as a bridge to help you to cross over from reading to practising. While reading will offer you some inspiration and encouragement, prayer will happen in the practising.

Some of the practices included here have been adapted from resources I first received on a retreat, during which my own understanding of prayer was punctured and I found myself staring wide-eyed with gratitude at the richness of the Christian tradition and its many approaches to prayer. Other practices have been taken or adapted from books, seminars and websites I have found nourishing, others still from conversations with friends. Many have been developed, extended or adapted from my own experience of playing in prayer. The selection I have included is not meant to demarcate what does and does not count as prayer. My hope is that these practices will open your eyes to what can become prayer when we approach life with open hearts and a desire to respond to God. You may find that one of these practices speaks right to where you are now; you may feel an instant attraction and glimpse a path forward. Or you may find that you are intrigued by a number of them and are drawn to experiment and play. You might also find that your prayer changes over time and that you become drawn to a practice you had originally discounted as not for you.

Before we continue, I want to emphasise that the playful approach to prayer offered in the pages ahead is not intended to be a rejection of established patterns of prayer or a devaluing of more disciplined approaches. Indeed, many of the practices I have included are ancient and only yield their fruit with patient repetition. My intention is not to replace or diminish an existing prayer life but to expand the parameters of prayer, by introducing some flexibility and openness. In my experience, taking a playful approach to praying sometimes encourages me to be open to making a change to my existing pattern of prayer by introducing new practices and sometimes it encourages me to persevere with existing practices or rhythms by helping me to be flexible with my expectations and open to staying with resistance. The playful approach is less about creating a program of prayer and more about nurturing a willingness to be guided deeper, however that may happen. It has room for both experiment and discipline and there is no need to choose. Whether you naturally favour the novel or the traditional, the disciplined or the wild, the planned or the surprising, I hope that exploring a playful approach to prayer will be both meaningful and helpful for you.

Section 1:
Reflections on
Playful Prayer

The Invitation to Pray

"If I were to be responsible for guiding souls, I would urge everyone to be aware of God's constant presence, if for no other reason than God's presence is a delight to our souls and spirit."   *-Brother Lawrence*

Picture the scene: it's a warm, sunny day and you are beside a vast lake. The sun is bright and strong but there's a cool, refreshing breeze to cut through the heat. The lake is twinkling in the sunlight, waves gently lapping the shore. There are children running in the shallows as they laugh and splash one another. Deeper out, a man is swimming, his head bobbing up and down. A woman floats on her back, eyes closed, buoyed by the gentle waves but otherwise still. Teenagers are throwing a ball to one another. A couple walk the shoreline, in step and hand in hand. A woman sits on the shore, head cast downwards. She digs her feet into the sand and allows the water to lap at her legs.

> I wonder what you notice about this image. What thoughts or feelings are stirred? How does your body respond? What draws you in? Does anything repel you? Where do you picture yourself in the scene?

For me, this is an abiding image of the freedom and spontaneity into which we are invited in prayer. It's an image of the invitation to enter the living water of God's abundantly available presence and pray as we are and not how we wish we were. This is the invitation to let go of shoulds and be with God in trust and vulnerable openness, bringing our energy and laughter, our weariness and our tears, our need for rest and play, our questions and doubts.

The choice of water imagery is not accidental. Throughout the Bible, water is used as a metaphor for God's Spirit and presence[1] and, in John's Gospel, Jesus' promises to give living water to all those who thirst.[2] In these passages, I hear Jesus promising not just enough water to quench thirst but an abundance of water: enough to well up within us and become a spring or a river, a source of life for us and for others.

It is into the abundance of God's presence that we are invited in prayer. Much as a vast lake welcomes all who seek to splash, float, swim and play so the living water of God is offered to all who come, whether tentative or confident, loud or quiet, restrained or wild. We can bring our words and our silence, our bodies and our feelings, our memories and imaginations, our creativity and our wounds. We can be ourselves right here, where we are now; all is welcome and we need not hold back or try to perform. And much as a lake holds water enough to refresh, cleanse, soothe and wash, so the living water of God's presence offers all the refreshment and healing that we need. It may take time and it may take some effort but all that our souls long for is already enfolded in a life of prayerful presence.

> *Much as a vast lake welcomes all who seek to splash, float, swim and play so the living water of God is offered to all who come, whether tentative or confident, loud or quiet, restrained or wild.*

---

[1] The Psalter is a rich source of such imagery. For example, see Psalm 42:2, Psalm 63:1 and Psalm 143:6.
[2] See John 4:10; 7:37-38.

For reflection

Take a moment to sit with the image of the lake and the invitation to enter the living water of God's presence. What thoughts or feelings or questions or bodily sensations do you notice?

If my wrestling sounds familiar, perhaps you've also experienced the accompanying sense of heaviness that comes with a struggle to pray. It's easy to think that struggling with prayer is a bad sign; an indication that it's not for us or that we're incapable of prayer or that God isn't really there. Maybe we feel inclined to give up altogether. Maybe we do give up for a while. But struggling with prayer puts us in good company. Even those held up as spiritual exemplars wrestled with prayer. The writings of spiritual greats such as C. S. Lewis, Mother Teresa and Henri Nouwen suggest that all of them experienced dryness or boredom in prayer at various points in their lives. Letters published after her death suggest that Mother Teresa's struggle to pray lasted for years. In these letters she repeatedly describes the "terrible darkness" within and the silence, emptiness and loneliness she experienced when trying to pray.[1] Some find it difficult to understand or accept the uncertainty and struggles of people they have placed on spiritual pedestals, but there is comfort here for those of us who know what it is to wrestle with prayer. Taken together, the experience and example of these complex figures suggests that having questions about or difficulties with prayer doesn't disqualify us from praying. In fact, the willingness of these figures to continue to show up in prayer even in times of doubt, emptiness or boredom is perhaps the best indication of the depth of their longing for the living water of God's presence.

> ...the desire to begin to pray is itself already a form of prayer...

Perhaps, though, your struggle to pray is less to persevere in an existing prayer life during hard times but rather to get started in the first place. Again, you are not alone. Jesus' own disciples seem to have been unsure how to begin, asking Jesus to teach them to pray as John the Baptist taught his disciples.[2] And even when Jesus gave them the prayer now called the "Our Father" or the "Lord's prayer"

---

[1] Mother Teresa and Brian Kolodiejchuk, *Come Be My Light* (London: Rider, 2008), 1.
[2] Luke 11:1

as well as many teachings about prayer, they still struggled to act on their desire to pray. The very last time they were alone with Jesus before his death, they continued to wrestle with prayer, falling asleep when Jesus had explicitly asked them to stay awake and pray with him.[3] Desiring to pray but struggling to begin does not, then, mean that the invitation to pray is not extended to you. Quite the opposite; the desire to begin to pray is itself already a form of prayer because all prayer is really an expression of our longing for God. To want to pray and to struggle to do so does not put you far from God; it puts you in the company of those closest to Jesus.

For reflection

Take some time to reflect on your own experiences. In what ways have you found prayer a struggle?

---

[3] Matthew 26:36-46

Prayer as Response

"I am sure as I live that nothing is so near to me as God. God is nearer to me than I am to myself; my existence depends on the nearness and closeness of God."   *-Meister Eckhart*

One of the things that has most helped me with my struggle to pray has been reconceiving prayer as a response to a presence already here rather than as an effort of will to gain the attention of someone "out there". To explain, let me take you back to my teens when, full of angst and earnestness, I attended a retreat. At one point we were invited to come forward to receive prayer and, feeling myself in need of inner healing and guidance, I shuffled apprehensively to the front. During this prayer I was given the image of a door with me on one side and God on the other. I was told that between me and the door were many heavy boxes and that I needed to move the boxes in order to open the door. I'm sure there was truth in this image; there of course were things I was clinging onto which needed to be released. But, unfortunately, I received this image as a sign that I wasn't worthy of relationship with God and that I needed to move the boxes before I could enter into that relationship. For a long time, prayer was hard. No matter how hard I tried, I couldn't shake the image of myself trying and failing to move the boxes, open the door and get to God. Eventually this image lost its intensity and was replaced with other images of relationship with God which opened up prayer in new ways. But from time to time, I would still think about the door.

One day my understanding of this image unexpectedly and suddenly shifted. Reading Henri Nouwen's *Here and Now*, I came across the following passage:

> "Once I saw a mime in which a man was straining to open one of the three doors in the room where he found himself. He pushed and pulled at the doorknobs, but none of the doors would open. Then he kicked with his feet against the

wooden panels of the door, but they didn't break. Finally, he threw his full weight against the doors but none of them yielded. It was a ridiculous, yet very hilarious sight, because the man was so concentrated on the three locked doors that he didn't notice that the room had no back wall and that he could simply walk out if he would only turn around and look!"[1]

Nouwen uses this as an image of inner transformation, of God's invitation to stop trying so hard to open locked doors and to turn around and find freedom. As I read his description of the mime, I was reminded of my image of the door and the boxes. In that moment, I realised that all that effort I'd been putting into moving those boxes was completely unnecessary. God was on the other side of the door, but God was also inside the room with me and had been all along. I suddenly realised I also had prayer upside down: it wasn't a task to be completed but a gift to be received. I'd been thinking of prayer as something I needed to do on my own effort instead of recognising it as a response to a presence already here.

> Our prayers don't make God come close; God is already closer to us than we can possibly imagine.

As long as we think of prayer as something we have to initiate, it will carry on being hard, if not impossible. The first step to becoming pray-ers is recognising that prayer is always a response to God. Our prayers don't make God come close; God is already closer to us than we can possibly imagine. What's more, God is constantly reaching out to us, seeking us out, inviting us deeper, gently nudging us to share whatever is held within our bodies, or on our minds, or in our hearts.

God's reaching, seeking, and inviting takes many forms. Sometimes we experience it through events in our lives: through fortuitous opportunities that may, on the surface, seem like

[1] Henri Nouwen, *Here and Now: Living in the Spirit* (New York: The Crossroad Publishing Company, 1994), 68-69.

coincidence, or through interruptions which may only be revealed as gifts when viewed in hindsight. Sometimes it's through nature: through the thrill of beautiful sunsets or intricate spider's webs or through the attention-capturing drama of thunderstorms or the wilderness. Sometimes it's through those around us: through kind words and generous actions. God's endless reaching out to us can even be experienced in or through painful situations. Not because God desires our suffering but because, in the middle of our suffering, we can experience a cracking open of hardened coping mechanisms, an unravelling of false self-identities, or a revealing of places in need of deep healing.

All of these, and more, are movements of God in our world and in us. They are invitations to respond to, and engage in, a conversation and relationship that is already happening within us at our deepest, soulful level. When we respond, and continue to respond to these movements, we allow the conversation and relationship to deepen and grow. It won't always be steady or smooth (what relationship or conversation is?) but it will be intimate and it will be authentically ours.

For reflection

What images underpin your understanding of prayer? Do these images help or hinder you in praying?

14

Prayer and Eros

"True whole prayer is nothing but love." -St Augustine

An invitation-and-response understanding of prayer is very different to the beaming-up model of prayer that might be more familiar to us. In this model of prayer, we shoot up requests to God who sits "up there" and decides whether or not to intervene based on whether it's the right kind of prayer or the right time or we're the right kind of person. An invitation-and-response understanding of prayer is more about our prayers echoing and deepening what is already being revealed within and around us. Through prayer, we open up to experiencing more of what God has lovingly revealed to us; we respond to the gentle movement of God towards us, and go deeper into the heart of things.

Shocking as it may sound, this understanding of prayer as desire returning desire, longing enfolded in longing can be appropriately described as erotic. Not because it has to do with the narrow range of things Western society refers to as "erotic" but because of its connection with the Greek understanding of eros (desire). In Greek philosophy, eros carries the sense of self-forgetful love running towards the other. Erotic prayer, then, is prayer that is a self-forgetful response to the invitation of a ceaselessly inviting and welcoming God. Erotic prayer is the beloved's response to the lover. On this understanding, God is not "up there" but already with, within and around us, even when life feels like a locked room or that we're staring at a huge pile of boxes. And our prayers don't "beam up" to God but take us beneath the surface of events or words or ourselves, helping us to become present to what's really going on and to discovering God already there in it.

This invitation-and-self-forgetful-response understanding of prayer is grounded in the theology of all three Abrahamic religions (Judaism, Christianity and Islam) but particularly the Christian doctrines of creation, incarnation and redemption. All three of these doctrines take as their starting point an understanding of God as not static or inert but the movement of love. In Eastern Orthodoxy, the life of God is described as a round dance (*perichoresis*) between the three persons of the Trinity, an image I love because of the communality and joy that it evokes. Creation happens because God's love overflows, not out of need but because of delight (if this is hard to understand, think about a time you've felt yourself bursting with joy). Creation, then, is an expression of divine love and all of creation is both enfolded by, and points back to, the round dance of love between the persons of the Trinity.

This sets the stage for prayer as response because all is sacred with each created thing containing a hidden pathway into the divine. In prayer, we say yes to moving along that path. But, according to Christian teaching, God doesn't leave us to walk the path alone. In the incarnation, God reaches out to creation definitively—

If prayer is creature and creator communing, then Jesus is prayer enfleshed.

putting on human flesh and dwelling among us, revealing what divine love in human form looks like. Through the incarnation, God brings our prayer to us, joining invitation with response. If prayer is creature and creator communing, then Jesus is prayer enfleshed. In his divine nature, Jesus embodies God's overflowing desire for us and, in his human nature, Jesus embodies our self-forgetful loving response. In his personhood, Jesus is the place where our longing for God and God's longing for us meet and it is as the meeting place between our longing for God and God's longing for us that Jesus is the embodiment of prayer. Through the incarnation, God brings our prayer to us, enrobed with flesh, showing us that God knows our struggles, our fears, our longings and that we don't need to hide or withdraw. Jesus' very being invites us to prayer and when we pray, we unite ourselves with him, joining his prayer to the Father.

To put this differently, through prayer we are caught up in the dynamic, dancing life of God. Jesus is both the revelation of God's longing for us to join the dance and the revelation of how we say yes to our longing to dance with God. Through his death and resurrection, Jesus mysteriously removes all barriers to our dancing with God by untangling our sin, by entering our pain and our despair, and by bringing the light of love to all places. This is the joy of Easter and this is the joy which we are invited to taste in prayer.

For reflection

How does this vision of prayer sit with you? Pay attention to thoughts, feelings and bodily sensations. What do you notice?

Growing Together as Pray-ers

"You don't think your way into a new way of living. You live your way into a new way of thinking."   -Richard Rohr

But *how* do we pray? Even when we let go of thinking of prayer as a performance or task and instead begin to see it as a response to the movement of God's love, we may still struggle to begin. No prayer seems to fit, no practice gets established, and we end up feeling guilty and frustrated. Or prayer works for a time and then dries up and feels hollow and empty and we don't know what to do. We want to get back, but we find that the old way seems to have closed and another has not yet appeared. Perhaps this sounds familiar.

Sometimes what's needed is the encouragement that it's enough simply to say whatever it is our hearts are prompting us to say or even not to speak at all, simply to be still. We need to be reassured that we don't need fancy words, or appropriate emotions, or to be the right sort of person. We don't earn the right to pray – it is a gift and one that is always available. But sometimes our desire for something more in prayer is fertile ground for discovering new practices – an invitation to expand our understanding of how prayer can look and feel. Often, I suspect, it's a mixture of both.

Fortunately, we have the benefit of millennia of thinking and advice on the topic of prayer. Even if we limit ourselves to a study of Christian tradition (which we don't need to do) we find a treasure trove of practices. These prayers and practices were developed to address just the sort of struggles we have and still have much to teach us. Together they form a rich well from which we may draw in our thirst for something more in our spiritual life. As we learn from those who go ahead of us, we're reminded that we are not alone in our quest for closeness in our relationship with God: many walk before us and encourage us to add our unique footprints to our shared journey as we grow together as pray-ers.

The invitation to join those who walk before and alongside us is open to all, irrespective of background or experience but it's easy to feel blocked in responding. We can remain trapped in the narrow confines of practices we have already received, clinging to them because they are familiar and seem safe even when they are no longer life-giving. Maybe we give lip service to the idea that prayer is open-ended and diverse but when we come to pray we slip back into our usual patterns because anything else seems strange and intimidating. There is, undoubtedly, value in persevering with patterns of prayer that hold special meaning or which we know to be deeply life-giving, even if we don't always come away feeling uplifted or instantly gratified. But if we're clinging to our patterns of prayer because we are afraid to try anything else or they continually leave us feeling dry and spiritually unfed, it may be time to explore another facet of the rich tradition we have inherited.

...we are not alone in our quest for closeness in our relationship with God...

This may feel like a bold or challenging step. Perhaps it means holding more loosely our assumptions about how prayer should or must look. Perhaps it means being willing to receive from people or groups we had previously discounted (or were told to discount). Perhaps it means letting the learning come through, rather than before, the process. Always it will mean saying yes to uncertainty, curiosity, and wonder. Always it will mean being willing to be a beginner.

For reflection

How do you tend to think prayer should look or feel? What would it be like to try something different?

Praying as Playing

"We don't stop playing because we grow old; we grow old because we stop playing." -George Bernard Shaw[1]

My daughter, Phoebe, was slow to speak and it took several years for anyone except me to understand her. Aged 4, she was still working on her articulation and particularly struggled with her Ls and Rs, pronouncing them both as a W. Context would usually help when trying to figure out what she was trying to say but it wasn't an exact science.

During a family visit my parents offered to put the children to bed. Everyone was happy with this arrangement: the children love their Nana and Grampy and my husband and I welcome any break we can get. Everything was going smoothly but after a while I noticed things had been quiet for quite a long time and I decided to go check if they needed anything. When I walked in I found my mum snuggled up with Phoebe. "Everything ok?" I asked. "Oh yes," Nana replied, "everything's fine. Phoebe just keeps wanting to pray".

Now, while Phoebe does enjoy praying, especially singing prayers, the whole situation seemed a bit off. "Is that right, Phoebe, you want to keep praying?" I asked. Phoebe suddenly sat up and declared in a loud voice "No, I want to PWAY. I want to pway with my dollhouse".

For Phoebe the similarity between play and pray is rooted in an approximation of letters which results in occasionally frustrating situations but in her book *Praying with Body and Soul*, Jane Vennard notices a deeper connection and argues that we miss out if we don't include play and humour in our prayers:

---

[1] This quote is widely attributed to George Bernard Shaw, but the accuracy of the attribution is ambiguous. In any case, the thought rings true.

"I understand 'sense of humour' to mean a light perspective on life, an ability to see the comic in creation and humanity, and a willingness to laugh at ourselves. Human relationships cannot survive without a sense of humour. Even when our relationships are difficult and uncomfortable and we have to 'work' on them to ease the struggles, clear the communication, allow ourselves to know and be known, we can laugh and discover the humour in our predicaments. So it is with our relationship with God. If all our prayers are solemn, all our conversations with God serious, all of our listening for God attuned to the 'important', we have missed the opportunity of light, silly, playful prayer. When we bring our humour to God with a sense of humour who knows what might happen next!"[2]

I appreciate this perspective and this book includes several of Vennard's prayer practices, but I think the connection between play and prayer goes even deeper. Whereas Vennard sees playful prayer as one component of our conversation with God, I think that true prayer always has a playful quality. Not because all prayer is light-hearted or joyful but because play and prayer require the same posture of openness, spontaneity and receptivity. As Troy Cady explains in his book *PlayFull*, playing is not a discrete set of activities reserved only for young people but a way of being present, a way of "giving yourself whole-heartedly to whatever life has to offer."[3]

To pray in a spirit of play is to give ourselves whole-heartedly to God.

Grounded in this understanding of play, a playful approach to prayer doesn't need to trivialise our prayer or place a limit on what we can bring in prayer. To play before God in prayer doesn't mean

---

[2] Jane Vennard, *Praying with Body and Soul: A Way to Intimacy with God* (Minneapolis: Augsburg, 1998), 63.
[3] Troy Cady, *PlayFull: Play as a Pathway to Personal & Relational Vitality* (Chicago: independently published, 2019), 185.

pretending to be sweet and innocent, bringing only our pleasant feelings and experiences. It neither denies the worth of prayer nor dishonours God. Instead, thinking of prayer as playful encourages us to take ourselves lightly by responding to God with honesty and curious wonder. Taking a playful approach to praying develops in us a confident trust that we can unselfconsciously bring our whole selves and that nothing has to be excluded. It nurtures our willingness to have a go, trust the process and see what happens. To pray in a spirit of play is to give ourselves whole-heartedly to God.

For reflection

What do you associate with the word "play"? Do you feel free to play in your prayer life?

24

Learning to Play and Pray

"It is a happy talent to know how to play." -Ralph Waldo Emerson[1]

I hope, in time, I can teach Phoebe the deeper connection between prayer and play so that she doesn't feel she needs to make a choice between playing and praying and can instead play with prayer and pray with play. But in learning how to practise playfulness, Phoebe and her brother Henry, have very much been my teachers, and I their student.

It wasn't always this way; I didn't always need help learning to play. As a child I was an expert too and my favourite games were imaginative and outdoorsy. In particular, I remember enjoying playing "the circus game" in the garden with my sisters. We would lay skipping ropes on the grass and pretend to walk a tightrope, we would swing and pretend to be acrobats, we would attempt to juggle pretending to be clowns. We'd lose track of time playing these games, completely absorbed in their unfolding.

I assumed that, because of my memories of playing, this part of parenting would be easy. In reality I've found the opposite. It's embarrassing to admit but I've found it hard to play with my children. I've found it difficult to resist my urge to want to achieve and be productive, to ignore the to-do list or laundry. I've also found it difficult to let go of being serious and sensible and relax into being silly and unpredictable. I have friends who have managed to carry the gift of play into their adult lives but, for me, I've found that gaining adult responsibilities, and accruing the skills needed to fulfil them, has meant losing an ease in play.

But, by watching my children I've slowly re-learnt how to play. It's been a work of letting go or, to use an expression from Ignatian spirituality, of "acting against" tendencies that lead us away from

---

[1] This quote is widely attributed to Ralph Waldo Emerson, but the accuracy of the attribution is ambiguous.

wholeness.[2] And it's the same work that's helped me to enjoy a more spontaneous and expansive prayer life.

The first step in learning to play and to pray has been letting go of my usual approach to time by refusing to let my life be governed by the clock. In the past, I've thought this is unavoidable and innocent - a natural consequence of trying to be a responsible member of a busy society. When I first heard prayer described as "wasting time with God"[3] I thought it was insulting to both God and time. But being tightfisted in my approach to time tends to make me anxious and fretful and far less present in any single moment of the day. And when I'm trying to squeeze the most out of each day, I tend not to have any time to play or pray: I'm far too wrapped up in my own agenda and with clock-watching to let myself be interrupted or waste time on something unplanned. Learning to play and pray has been a work of learning to hold time more lightly, of saying no to judging my worth by how much I can do in any given period and of seeing intentionally wasted time with both my children and with God as something to celebrate not berate.

Learning to play and pray has also meant acting against my tendency to feel I need to act a certain part. I've had to let go of trying to be a tidy version of myself in order to just be for a while, whether that's agreeing to Phoebe's request that I crawl around like a dog or letting myself linger under a tree and consider it prayer. It can be uncomfortable to be responsive and spontaneous like this but there's an honesty in it that is deeply freeing. In prayer, that freedom can feel like a release of trying to sound clever or have more noble feelings or be more loving or be more like someone else. Sometimes what is expressed is raw and wounded (maybe we're even a bit shocked or embarrassed afterwards) but, even then, there's a healing that comes from letting go of shoulds, or of trying to maintain an image at any cost. As Jesus teaches in the parable of the

---

[2] For an introduction to Ignatian acting against see Margaret Silf, *Inner Compass: An Invitation to Ignatian Spirituality* (Chicago: Loyola Press, 1999), 104.
[3] See Henri Nouwen, *Spiritual Formation: Following the Movements of the Spirit* (London: SPCK, 2011), 19-20.

tax collector and the Pharisee, prayer isn't about establishing or maintaining an image but about honesty and vulnerability.[4]

Also unhelpful when it comes to prayer or play is a resistance to repetition. Anyone who has played with very young children will know how repetitive their play can be. Stacking, counting, lining up blocks again and again featured highly when my children were tiny. Even imaginative games seemed to entail a lot of repetition. When Henry and Phoebe were preschoolers, I lost count of the number of ice-cream cones I ordered from their make-believe shop. Looking back, I see the beauty in the slowness but I confess that, at the time, I found it all a bit tedious. I'd notice how strong my urge was to move things along or mix things up.

In prayer, too, I've noticed I naturally resist repetition. I'm unwilling to say or do the same things too often. I suppose it's partly because I don't like to admit how simple and few my deepest thoughts and wants really are. It might also be because I have a lingering fear that God will be irritated by too much of the same thing. I

...in prayer, as in play, repetition is not only tolerated but critical.

remember a friend telling me about a difficult situation in her life and her adding, as a throwaway comment, that she wasn't going to pray about it any more because she'd already prayed about it and now she needed to have faith and wait. She seemed sad as she said this and my heart was heavy for her because I could feel how hard she was working on not doing the thing she really wanted to do. She seemed lonely and I wondered if it was needless, especially since Jesus teaches that it's repetition in prayer, not restraint, that is the true marker of faithfulness.[5] And yet, I also recognise myself in her resistance. I know that it's hard to let go of feeling I need to make progress or that I should wait with a stiff upper lip. It can be hard to let myself be, or sound, repetitive. But slowly, I'm accepting that in prayer, as in play, repetition is not only tolerated but critical. To be truly honest with God we have to be honest with ourselves and go on

---

[4] Luke 18:9-14
[5] Luke 18:1-8

27

and on and on about the same things and practise again and again and again the things that nourish us. We don't need to manage the process; all we need to do is to keep noticing and responding to what's happening around and within. We can be as predictable as we like.

For reflection

What helps you to play?

The Goal of Prayer

"Prayer enlarges the heart until it is capable of containing God's gift of Himself."   *-Mother Teresa*

I hope that it is becoming clearer that this understanding of prayer as rooted in desire returning desire is about responding to a presence already there and that you are free to respond however you feel led. There is no need to perform, compare or strive. The invitation is for you, exactly as you are; healthy growth comes in, not before, the response. You can be yourself and you are welcome to bring the full spectrum of your experience, thoughts and emotions; all can be part of a loving response to love's invitation.

Perhaps, though, you're wondering what the point is of praying in this way or how you'll know if you're doing it right.

These questions may feel particularly pressing if you're familiar with or, perhaps, haunted by, the beaming up model of prayer in which pray-ers shoot requests up to a God "out-there" who demands our attention. According to this understanding of prayer, we pray because we're supposed to pray and also because it's a way to get the things we want. The goal is to gain God's attention and favour and the success of our prayer is measured by whether or not we receive the things, results or feelings we've asked for.

This understanding of prayer is deeply problematic, not least because it is more transactional than relational. God takes on the character of a shopkeeper, with our prayers our currency for getting what we want. On such a model, it's only worth praying if we get what we're seeking. When prayers aren't, or don't seem to be, answered, it makes sense to give up.

In contrast, an invitation and response model of prayer has no goal except the ongoing relationship with God, which it helps to deepen. Prayer nourishes the loving relationship between soul and God. Prayer is how we say yes to being caught up in the flow of God's love and how we begin to see things from within that love. Through

29

prayer, we allow ourselves to be loved by God and through surrender to that love, become aligned with the movement of God's love in the world. As Julian of Norwich writes: "The fruit and the end of our prayers... [is that] we be oned and like to our Lord in all things."[1]

> *Prayer is how we say "yes" to being caught up in the flow of God's love and how we begin to see things from within that love.*

The sign of a fruitful prayer life will not be a specific answer or feeling but an increase in embodied loving action in the world that seems to organically overflow from our loving relationship with God. As we come to know we are loved, just as we are, we are freed to love others, just as they are. This isn't a sentimental feeling that whitewashes injustice but a deep awareness of the gratuitous love that holds and anchors all and which makes every creature deserving of our attention and care. Precisely what this embodied loving action will look like will depend on where, when, and with whom we live, as well as the unique gifting we have, but it will always move us towards becoming more humane, less preoccupied with shoring up things and experiences for ourselves and more concerned with honouring the deep bonds between us as interconnected, beloved creatures. For Christians, Jesus' life offers the definitive example and model.

None of this, however, is to say that we shouldn't ask God for the things that we want, either for ourselves or for others. Jesus is clear that it is good to ask God for our hearts' deepest desires and to be persistent in asking.[2] Naming what we want both flows from and grows openness and honesty and these things are critical for any relationship, including relationship with God. We just have to be aware of when our honest requests are becoming manipulative demands, with each one a little test of how much God cares for us or even if God exists at all. I think this happens to most of us, at some point or other, and it can be difficult to notice it, let alone choose

---

[1] Julian of Norwich, *Revelations of Divine Love* (London: Penguin, 1998), XLII, 101.
[2] Luke 18:1-8

another response. But it is possible to do both and, in the garden of Gethsemane, Jesus shows us how. In this intensely honest prayer, Jesus models how we can acknowledge and express our fears and desires while keeping the relationship as the real goal of prayer. Faced with imminent arrest, torture and execution, Jesus prays that the cup of suffering be taken from him but then, startlingly, he adds "yet not my will but yours".[3]

In the Gospels these petitions form one sentence but I've often wondered how long it took to move from one to the other and what that spiritual journey was like. In the past, I saw the movement from "take this cup" to "your will be done" as one of inner wrestling, a sort of zero-sum game in which only one desire could win. I saw this prayer as one of self-sacrifice and marvelled at the spiritual courage and effort it must have taken. Over time, though, I've begun to see it slightly differently; not so much as a movement of overcoming self but as a prayer of radical trust in God's love. The self-surrender is still there but it's less the result of mental or even spiritual effort and more the result of a willingness to stay with his anxiety and fear and allow it to be completely enfolded and directed by divine love. Between "take this cup" and "your will be done" Jesus moves deeper into his trust in God and finds that it is strong enough to include even the anguish of what is to come. It reminds me of a prayer of Henri Nouwen:

> "Dear God, I so much want to be in control. I want to be the master of my own destiny. Still I know that you are saying: 'Let me take you by the hand and lead you. Accept my love and trust that where I will bring you, the deepest desires of your heart will be fulfilled.' Lord, open my hands to receive your gift of love. Amen."[4]

In Gethsemane, then, Jesus models how to let a loving relationship with God be both the beginning and the end of prayer.

---

[3] Luke 22:42
[4] Henri Nouwen, *With Open Hands* (Notre Dame: Ave Maria, 2006), 62.

The trust which he enters through prayer is a deepening of the trust that begins his prayer. This trust doesn't obliterate anxiety or fear but provides a holding space for all thoughts, feelings and physical sensations so they do not overwhelm or consume, even when they are honestly faced.

But as much as we may want to discover those deeper, truer desires or to deepen our trust in God's love, we don't need to be in a rush. It may take a long time for us to move from "take this cup" to "not my will but yours". We begin where we are and let ourselves be moved deeper by the love that guides us. We can trust the process; we don't need to hurry it along or try to manage it. We will never be more loved than we are right now. While some reflection is natural and healthy, it's more important to keep praying, however and whenever you feel led. God will guide you into the rest.

As Herbert McCabe writes:

> "In true prayer you must meet God and meet yourself where you really are, for it is just by this that God will move you on...When as honestly as you can you speak to God of your desires, very gently and tactfully [God] will often reveal to you that in fact you have deeper and more mature desires. But there is only one way to find this out: to start from where you are."[5]

For reflection

What are your expectations or hopes about prayer?

---

[5] Herbert McCabe, *God, Christ and Us* (London: Bloomsbury, 2005), 105.

Pause

Before you read on, I invite you to return to the image with which this section began. Picture, again, the lake twinkling in the sunlight and the diversity of those in and beside the water. As the scene forms in your imagination, what do you notice? How do you want to respond? Do you feel welcome or out of place? Do you want to join in or walk away? Gently acknowledge whatever comes. Do not try to force anything or ignore resistance.

When you feel ready to read on, my hope is that you will cast your eyes over the following chapters in the way you might cast your eyes over that friendly lakeshore. May you smile at the variety of practices in the way you might smile at those laughing and splashing and playing in the water. May you delight in the diversity of pathways to encounter with God and feel the invitation to join in, trusting that God's love and presence welcomes your unique expression. May your eyes and ears be opened to see and hear God's invitation to you. Whether you dip your toes in or throw yourself in head-first, whether you come with tears to be washed or with laughter and a sense of fun or with a quiet yet urgent longing for more, may you sense God's invitation is for you, now, just as you are.

Section 2:
Practising a Playful
Prayer Life

Praying with Scripture

For those who give priority to both Scripture and prayer, it can be easy to think of reading Scripture and praying as separate items on a spiritual checklist. Have I read my Bible? Have I prayed? Perhaps we also try to take our spiritual temperature by getting a sense of how often we are completing these tasks. Perhaps we add other tasks to the checklist - attending church, for example, or quiet time or going on a retreat.

At its best, this checklist mentality is rooted in a desire to be spiritually healthy, a longing for a strong relationship with God that will anchor us and enable us to weather life's storms. We know that if we want our bodies to be healthy, we need to eat a balanced diet and exercise, and similarly, we sense that for our souls to be healthy we need to practise regularly those things that help us to connect with God and our belovedness.

But the checklist mentality is inherently problematic. When I'm asked about how often I pray or read my Bible or complete any other spiritual task I can't help but feel one of two things: either a pang of shame because, on reflection, I haven't been very disciplined, or pride because I've been doing well. Neither one is helpful. Whatever my response, these questions shift the focus from God's presence and invitation to my behaviour and performance. I'm left feeling inadequate and discouraged or, worse, smug and complacent. Neither of these postures encourages vulnerable openness to divine love.

Not only does the checklist approach tend to hinder spiritual growth by placing the emphasis in the wrong place, but it also tends to block a rich and interconnected spiritual life. In this model, reading Scripture and praying are offered as separate activities to be approached one at a time instead of being positioned as entwined and mutually supportive.

This doesn't mean that Scripture can only be explored within a prayerful context or that prayer must be joined with reading Scripture. Both prayer and Scripture are gifts and there is freedom to explore both as yourself and in the place you find yourself. Shoulds and shouldn'ts move us into a shame/pride dichotomy; gentleness and playfulness are better guides. If praying with Scripture doesn't draw you at this time, you don't need to force it.

The interconnectedness of Scripture and prayer is not, then, a barrier or limit. It's an invitation to approach both prayer and Scripture in deeper and more expansive ways. When allowed to flow into one another, they enrich each other and offer fruitful ways of responding to God.

On one hand, Scripture opens up prayer and in several ways. First, Scripture teaches us how to pray with words by giving us words we can speak back to God. Reading Scripture we discover that we don't need to invent our own ways of speaking to God, we don't need to be anxious about what words to use but we can join our prayers with those of others. We find that the Bible is crammed full of all sorts of word-filled prayers; prayers of thanksgiving and joy, prayers of confession and repentance, prayers of hope and trust, prayers of liberation and healing. Certain books of the Bible are key here—in particular, the Psalms—but there are prayers scattered throughout Scripture. Any cry, shout or whisper to God, indeed any expression of longing for God, is a prayer.

> *When we pray with Scripture, we're joined with others in our longing to respond to God and we discover companions for our journey deeper into communion with God.*

Joining our prayers with those of others not only relieves our anxiety or uncertainty about what to say but also connects us to a praying people. When we pray with Scripture, we're joined with others in our desire to respond to God and we discover companions for our journey deeper into communion with God. This awareness of being connected can help us to persevere when prayer feels hard or unfulfilling. We know we're not alone.

Grounding this connection as a praying people is a shared story and it's this story that Scripture seeks to tell. Reading Scripture deepens prayer by reminding us that our seemingly separate lives are part of a cosmic tapestry that reveals the intimate interweaving of God and creation. Our lives are no less meaningful or significant for this growth in awareness. Rather, this rooting gives us a new perspective on our struggles and joys: they aren't simply our own but flecks in the fabric of the larger, unfolding story of God's people. This is both humbling and affirming. We find ourselves situated in a living faith that stretches before and beyond us, reminding us that we seek God in community and are called to seek the renewal of all creation.

On the other hand, prayer opens onto Scripture and, again, it does this in several ways. First, prayer opens up the Bible in a new way. Approached prayerfully, the Bible is no longer simply a book of information about what people believe God has done and wants us to do in response but becomes a source of deep, spiritual nourishment. Scripture offers itself not simply as food for our inquiring minds but for our whole selves. Recognising this helps us to hear what Scripture has to say, not only to our desire for answers and understanding but also to the deep places in us which long for healing, forgiveness and love. We bring our full selves to Scripture and allow God to touch us in our reading.

Approaching Scripture in prayer also positions us correctly to read Scripture. When we come to Scripture in prayer, we allow our faith to lead. We're no longer seeking proof texts to back up our rationally argued positions but instead seeking understanding for the gift of our faith. This is a position of openness and trust rather than suspicion and self-righteousness. It means we allow ourselves to be surprised by what we find and to trust that the living Word present in Scripture has infinite depth and the power to speak to each of us. This doesn't relativise truth but rather honours the transcendence of God. After all, the Bible doesn't contain God but opens onto God, as both a record of divine encounters and a place for encounter. Praying with Scripture enables us to hear the living

Word speaking to us through the words of Scripture: to participate in the relationship with God to which all of Scripture points. Through this experience we learn to approach Scripture with an expansive reverence rather than a neat and tidy certainty.

The interconnectedness of prayer and Scripture is a gift to anyone struggling with prayer or, indeed, with Scripture. Rather than seeing prayer and reading Scripture as two separate tasks to be completed in order to be spiritually successful, we can see them as interconnected openings onto deeper relationship with God. We can pray with Scripture and read Scripture prayerfully. What's more, this interplay between Scripture and prayer, can open us up to hearing from and responding to God in other ways. In other words, praying with Scripture doesn't diminish or replace other ways of praying but can help us better to listen to God's movement and Word in all areas of life.

My own experience of learning to pray with Scripture and to read Scripture prayerfully has been slow and undulating. Partly this is due to religious trauma. Like many, I have experienced Scripture being used as a weapon, a way of dismissing, condemning or shaming those who are regarded as somehow lesser, unworthy or dangerous. Sometimes my Bible has seemed to symbolise the confident assertions of the self-proclaimed "righteous" and it has been a challenge to open my Bible with genuine vulnerability and trust. I have struggled to believe that I will hear the voice of love and not that of oppression.

It was also hard to pray with my Bible because I simply didn't know where to start. Which book or chapter to read? How much is enough? How can I be sure that my reading is prayerful? The first step has been to loosen my grip on these questions and to recognise that if my intention is to draw closer to God then my efforts will be enough and my reading will automatically have a prayerful quality. The second step has been to thankfully acknowledge that I walk a well-trodden path and I have many guides to help me navigate Scripture prayerfully. While there has been some temptation at this point to focus my efforts on finding the "right" way, there has also been freedom in discovering the range of fruitful ways in which others have approached Scripture and which remain open for me.

It's important, then, to recognise that the invitation to play with prayer also applies to Scripture. We may feel uncomfortable about playing with Scripture, but I suspect this says as much about our understanding of play as it does about our understanding of Scripture. The spontaneity and freedom that play evokes doesn't entail triviality but is a gateway to heart-centred encounter and transformation. Playing

Playing with Scripture means approaching it willing to be open and receptive, to try something new and to stay present to the process rather than seeking a particular outcome.

with Scripture means approaching it willing to be open and receptive, to try something new and to stay present to the process rather than seeking a particular outcome. And just as there are many ways to play, there are many ways to pray with Scripture. You may enjoy them all equally or you may feel more led in one direction.

The direction in which I have found myself most frequently led to play prayerfully with Scripture is by praying the daily Gospel. This is a traditional Roman Catholic, Anglican and Orthodox practice in which an assigned passage from the Gospels is offered for the Church to pray together along with passages from the Old Testament, New Testament and Psalms. The passages are compiled in a lectionary, which details the readings for each day of the liturgical year. While the passages chosen for each day vary between denominations, they are almost always brief and limited to a few verses.

Although I wasn't raised in a denomination that encouraged daily reading of assigned Biblical passages, I have found myself drawn to those traditions that have a lectionary because they offer companionship in reading Scripture prayerfully. There is something both comforting and humbling in having the decision about what to read that day made for me and knowing that others are reading the same passages as I am. Initially, I tried to read all the assigned passages for the day, but this left me feeling hurried and overwhelmed. I would come to the text as seekers came to the desert fathers and mothers of the third century hungry for "a word" to taste, eat and digest but would leave overfed with indigestion.

Eventually, I felt able to accept the invitation to simplify my practice and began to spend more time with the daily Gospel. Part of me wondered if this was lazy but another part recognised that the longing for "a word" was really a longing to hear the voice of Jesus. In a loud and frantic world, in which many voices demand my attention, it felt good to get quiet and to listen for just one voice. It was like finding a touchstone, a firm foundation on which all my other spiritual practices could be built.

Because the daily Gospel is short, I have time to savour the words fully, to notice their tone and texture. I chew on them through the day, slowly absorbing their meaning and allowing them to touch my inner being. Even when I hear challenge in them, this slow way of reading, of hearing Jesus' voice, allows me to notice my discomfort and resistance and leaves room to pray with it. I don't always receive insights, but I find that if I can avoid the temptation to move onto a more comforting passage to alleviate my discomfort and can pray with that discomfort, a next step presents itself. Often that step is to keep listening, remain attentive, wait in the uncertainty, try to be as open as possible, trusting God is moving in the space I seek to hold open.

This way of reading the daily Gospel is rooted in the ancient practice of *lectio divina*, a slow and contemplative way of reading Scripture in which we listen for the words that stand out or "shimmer", trusting that this isn't a coincidence but an invitation to listen further. Repetition is key to *lectio divina*, with the Cistercian monk, Michael Casey, describing repetition as the "soul" of genuine *lectio*.[1]

---

[1] Michael Casey, *Sacred Reading: The Ancient Art of Lectio Divina* (Liguori, MO: Triumph Books, 1996), 24.

Unlike most of our reading, in which we proceed in a linear way, *lectio divina* asks us to receive the text in a circular way, giving ourselves more time and space to notice what is being offered to us and to allow that noticing to settle deeper within. As Robert Mulholland explains in his book *Shaped by the Word*, this isn't an informational way of reading Scripture in which we try to bring the text under our control but a formational way of reading Scripture in which we open ourselves to be directed by the text.[2] In *lectio*, we let the text speak to us, and trust our deepest selves to notice and be transformed by the words they hold for us. Through *lectio* we allow God within to recognise and respond to God in the words of Scripture.

I've also found that certain passages ask to be read using my imagination and senses, using a practice called Gospel contemplation. This practice, developed by Ignatius of Loyola in the 16th century, uses imagination as a pathway into scenes from Jesus' life and can help the pray-er to receive Jesus' life and teachings in a more immediate way. Ignatius developed or, perhaps more accurately, discovered this way of praying with Scripture during a difficult transitional time in his life when his old way of being in the world seemed closed and a new way had not opened. As Margaret Silf explains:

> "[Ignatius] began to find himself, in imagination, present in scenes, conversations, and stories of the Gospels, and he began to participate in the plots of these stories. It was the start, for him, of an adventure into imaginative prayer that was to become a most powerful catalyst for the growth of this personal relationship with God, a method of prayer that is just as vividly available to us today."[3]

---

[2] M. Robert Mulholland, Jr., *Shaped by the Word: The Power of Scripture in Spiritual Formation* (Nashville: Upper Room, 1985), 50.
[3] Margaret Silf, *Inner Compass: An Invitation to Ignatian Spirituality* (Chicago: Loyola Press, 1999), xxi.

This "vividly available" method of prayer can be used with any scriptural passage but is best suited to action passages in which Jesus' actions or expressions are centre stage. By using our imaginations and senses to enter the scene, we open ourselves to encounter Jesus in a fresh, more visceral way. In my experience, it can be hard to suspend disbelief, to release my suspicion that I am too far removed from the scene to enter it in a meaningful way, to let go of my doubts that this is simply a version of wish fulfilment. Yet, when I am able to do this, it is as though a veil is pierced and I can attend to Jesus and those with him in a raw, unfiltered way. I am cracked open to receive the scenes and words as, in some way, for me and can respond more wholeheartedly and with embodied action.

While *lectio divina* and gospel contemplation have been particularly important as practices in my own prayer life and in the praying history of the church, they keep company with many other prayerful approaches to Scripture. Included below, alongside *lectio divina* and gospel contemplation, are practices centred around the Lord's Prayer, the Psalms and the Jesus Prayer, as well as invitations to join the prayer of a biblical character and to pray Scripture as a refrain through the day. All of these are offered as pathways into a deeper, more prayerful way of engaging with Scripture and, as you read on, I encourage you to notice what draws your attention and prompts a response. Perhaps you will find refreshment for an established practice or the inspiration for a new way of engaging Scripture prayerfully. Either way, I hope that this array of practices may help to widen your perspective on both Scripture and prayer and will serve as a window through which you might glimpse the marvellous possibilities that come from allowing Scripture and prayer to unlock each other as you move deeper into relationship with Emmanuel, God with you.

Do you tend to see prayer and reading Scripture as two separate tick boxes?

When, in your own personal prayer life, have you experienced Scripture and prayer opening onto each other?

What might be your barriers to praying with Scripture?

PRAYING THE OUR FATHER

When the disciples asked Jesus to teach them to pray, this was how Jesus responded (Luke 11:1). The gift of this prayer is offered to all who seek to pray; it's accessible yet with a depth of meaning that invites lifelong meditation. Praying this prayer will centre and nourish you at every stage of your spiritual journey and will also ground you in community with the whole praying body of Christ across time and space. Even if you already know and pray this prayer, you may be so familiar with its words that you speak them without pausing to let them speak to you. Perhaps the words remain at the surface of your awareness and don't make a home in your heart. If this resonates, one way to receive the gift of this prayer afresh is to slow down, pause to meditate on each line and listen for what God is inviting you to pay attention to today. It may also be helpful to read the prayer in an unfamiliar or less familiar translation or as an adaptation; you can find an example of the latter below.

Practising
~ Decide which translation you will use. If you are already familiar with this prayer and are seeking to connect with it more deeply, consider using a less familiar translation or an adaptation.

~ Begin by centering yourself in your intention to be present to this prayer. Depending on where you are, that might mean taking some deep breaths, or closing your eyes or planting your feet firmly on the ground.

~ Read or speak the words slowly and pause after each line, allowing the words to settle. You may like to visualise the words sinking deeper into your centre, like a pebble dropping into a body of water. You don't need to analyse them or force meaning; notice what thoughts or feelings are stirred but resist any urge to cling to them. Let these thoughts and feelings be like the ripples made by the pebble dropping into water.

~ When you reach the end of the prayer, allow yourself some time to simply be, just as you might wait for the surface of the water to become still again before dropping in another pebble.

~ Repeat this process as many times as you like.

~ Either end your prayer here or allow yourself some time to reflect on the following questions:

Which word, phrase or petition stands out today? What seems familiar in these words or in your response to them? What seems new or different? Are any of these words hard to pray today?

~ Offer these thoughts to God or simply sit in silence and know that Jesus prays for you always, even when praying is difficult for you.

The Lord's Prayer, an adaptation

"Eternal Spirit,
Earth-Maker, Pain-bearer, Life-giver
Source of all that is and all that shall be,
Father and Mother of us all,
Loving God who is in heaven:
The hallowing of your name echo through the universe!
The way of your justice be followed by people of the world!
Your heavenly will be done by all created beings!
Your commonwealth of peace and freedom sustain our
     hope and come on earth.
With bread we need for today, feed us.
In the hurts we absorb from one another, forgive us.
In times of temptation and test, strengthen us.
From trials too great to endure, spare us.
From the grip of all that is evil, free us.

For you reign in the glory of the power that is love, now and forever.
May it be so. Amen."

- from *The New Zealand Prayer Book*[4]

---

[4] See page 181 at https://anglicanprayerbook.nz/167.html (accessed 4 April, 2022)

JOINING THE PRAYER OF A BIBLICAL CHARACTER

If you struggle to find the words to pray, it can be helpful to join the prayer of a biblical character. Whatever life-event or emotion you are bringing in prayer, you can be sure that you aren't the first one to do so. The Bible is full of colourful characters and their prayers, and all are waiting to companion you in bringing your experiences to God. The following are extracts from a selection of biblical prayers, and I've chosen *The Message* translation for these passages to make the language more accessible. There are many more prayers woven through Scripture and if you enjoy praying in this way, you may like to create your own list of biblical prayers. Try joining your voice to these prayers, paying attention to where your own situation or that of those around you may connect or diverge. Consider replacing names or places with ones that resonate in your own life.

Practising

~ Scan through the prayers below and notice if there seems to be any resonance with what you feel drawn to pray for or about.

~ Read the prayer silently or aloud.

~ Pay attention to where your own situation or that of those around you may connect.

~ Read the prayer again, this time replacing names or places with ones that resonate in your own life. You may like to write out the new prayer. Be as creative as you feel led, treating the biblical passage as a springboard for your own expression of thought or emotion or bodily sensation to God.

Daniel's prayer of confession (Daniel 9:4-19)

"'O... God...we have sinned in every way imaginable. We've done evil things, rebelled, dodged and taken detours around your clearly marked paths...You have done everything right, Master, but all we have to show for our lives is guilt and shame, the whole lot of us... Oh yes, God, we've been exposed in our shame, all of us...before the whole world. And deservedly so, because of our sin. Compassion is our only hope, the compassion of you, the Master, our God, since in our rebellion we've forfeited our rights...So listen, God, to this determined prayer of your servant. Have mercy on your ruined Sanctuary. Act out of who you are, not out of what we are...Turn your ears our way, God, and listen....We know that we don't deserve a hearing from you. Our appeal is to your compassion. This prayer is our last and only hope."

Moses' prayer for mercy (Exodus 32:11-3)

"Why, God, would you lose your temper with your people? Why, you brought them out of Egypt in a tremendous demonstration of power and strength. Why let the Egyptians say, 'He had it in for them—he brought them out so he could kill them in the mountains, wipe them right off the face of the Earth.' Stop your anger. Think twice about bringing evil against your people! Think of Abraham, Isaac, and Israel, your servants to whom you gave your word, telling them 'I will give you many children, as many as the stars in the sky, and I'll give this land to your children as their land forever.'"

Mary's prayer of thanksgiving (Luke 1:46-49)

"I'm bursting with God-news; I'm dancing the song of my Savior God. God took one good look at me, and look what happened— I'm the most fortunate woman on earth! What God has done for me will never be forgotten, the God whose very name is holy, set apart from all others. His mercy flows in wave after wave on those who are in awe before him....It's exactly what he promised, beginning with Abraham and right up to now."

A tearful prayer for help with doubt (Mark 9:24)
"I believe. Help me with my doubts"

The centurion's prayer for healing (Matthew 8:8)
"Just give the order and [they] will be fine."

Jesus' prayer of surrender (Luke 22:42)
"Father, remove this cup from me. But please, not what I want. What do you want?"

Jesus' prayer of forgiveness (Luke 23:34)
"Father, forgive them; they don't know what they're doing."

Paul's prayer for wisdom and revelation for God's people (Ephesians 1:15-19)
"[I give thanks for you] But I do more than thank. I ask—ask the God of our Master, Jesus Christ, the God of glory—to make you intelligent and discerning in knowing him personally, your eyes focused and clear, so that you can see exactly what it is he is calling you to do, grasp the immensity of this glorious way of life he

has for his followers, oh, the utter extravagance of his
work in us who trust him—endless energy, boundless
strength!"

THREE WAYS TO PRAY THE PSALMS

The book of Psalms is the Bible's prayer book. To read the Psalms
with your heart open to God is to pray. Jesus referenced the Psalms
throughout his life (for example, Matthew 21:42, Mark 14:20-21,
Luke 23:46) and on the cross he prayed at least two Psalms. His
words "My God, my God, why have you forsaken me" (Matthew
27:46) are the first words of Psalm 22. He also prayed Psalm 31:5
when he called out in a loud voice, "Father, into your hands I commit
my spirit." (Luke 23:46) While Jesus never directly instructed the
disciples to pray the Psalms, it's telling that in his hour of greatest
need and human vulnerability, it was the Psalms to which Jesus
turned. Also, I'm not the first to notice that the prayer Jesus gave his
disciples - the Our Father or Lord's Prayer - seems to draw out some
of the main themes of the Psalms, as though Jesus was offering them
a condensed psalter. In his book on the Psalms, Dietrich Bonhoeffer
affirms with Martin Luther that the Psalter and the Lord's Prayer
interpenetrate "so that it is possible to understand one on the basis
of the other and to bring them into joyful harmony."[5]

If you let them, the Psalms will teach you how to bring your
whole self to God, including the full gamut of your emotions,
including the darker ones that you might try to hide, resist or
repress. John Calvin called the Psalter "An Anatomy of the Soul"
because "there is not an emotion of which anyone can be conscious

---

[5] Dietrich Bonhoeffer, *Psalms: The Prayer Book of the Bible* (Minneapolis:
Augsburg, 1970), 16.

that is not here represented as in a mirror."[6] The Psalms will encourage you to be honest in prayer as well as give you words to express yourself when you struggle to find your own. They also invite you to join your prayers with those of others, in different circumstances and emotional states, expanding your range of vision and deepening your understanding and compassion.

There are many ways to pray the Psalms; the following are some suggestions to get you started.

Practising

A. Praying a Psalm a day.

~ This is an adaptation of the sequential method of praying the Psalms encouraged by Eugene H. Peterson in *Answering God.*[7] This simple approach will allow your prayer life to be nourished by a full diet of Psalms.

~ Start with Psalm 1 and pray it – or a portion of it – either once or several times, for example, in the morning, afternoon, and evening (Psalm 55:17 suggests this practice).

~ As you pray the Psalm, listen for what stands out to you. It may be a word, phrase or image (as in the practice of *lectio divina*, also included in this chapter). Receive whatever presents itself as a word for you to be carried with you throughout your day. When you find yourself thinking about the word or image, try to maintain a posture of openness and curiosity, offering any thoughts or questions

---

[6] John Calvin, *Commentary on Psalms, volume 1* (Grand Rapids, MI: William B. Eerdmans Publishing Co., 1949), xxxvii.
[7] "That's it: open our Bibles to the book of Psalms and pray them - sequentially, regularly, faithfully across a lifetime. This is how most Christians for most of the Christian centuries have matured in prayer. Nothing fancy. Just do it." Eugene H. Peterson, *Answering God: The Psalms as Tools for Prayer* (New York: Harper One, 1989), 7.

to God. Avoid putting pressure on yourself to try to make sense of it or fit it neatly into your existing understanding.

~ The next day, move to Psalm 2. Pray through all 150 Psalms and then start over.

~ Don't worry if you miss a day; just pick up where you left off last time.

~ Even if the Psalm does not match your mood, know that it does match someone's mood today. Offer it as a prayer for them, rejoicing with those who rejoice and mourning with those who mourn.

B. Praying the Psalms through your emotions

~ This method is inspired by Walter Brueggemann's *Praying the Psalms* and offers a way to pray with and through emotion in communion with the psalmist.[8]

~ Allow yourself some time to notice and name the emotion or emotions you are feeling today. Depending on your personality this may be easy or challenging. If you find it very difficult, it may be helpful to move to the next step and let that assist you in naming your emotion.

~ Scan through the key to the Psalms and emotions included below and choose a Psalm that corresponds with your emotion.

---

[8] "The Psalms do not insist that we follow word-for-word and line-by-line, but they intend us to have great freedom to engage our imagination toward the Holy God. Our listening mostly moves in and out by a free association of ideas" Walter Brueggemann, *Praying the Psalms: Engaging Scripture and the Life of the Spirit* (Eugene: Cascade Books, 2007), 27.

~ Read that Psalm, allowing it to express your emotion. As much as you are able, give yourself permission to express your emotions as you read, for example, with laughter, tears, raised voice, sighs.

~ Let this experience guide you in finding your own words to express your emotion, either incorporating this as you pray through the Psalm or adding it at the end.

C. Paraphrasing a Psalm

~ This method is modelled by Malcolm Guite in his book *David's Crown*.[9] Here Guite offers 150 poems, each one a prayerful response to a Psalm and each one beginning with the last line of the one before so that together they form a crown. Guite is a skillful poet but that doesn't qualify him to paraphrase the Psalms; far more important is his willingness to respond to the Psalms' invitation to express himself creatively to God. You don't need to be a poet to access this way of praying and your Psalm can be as simple or complex as you like. The most important thing is to be yourself and to use the language that is meaningful to you. This method is compatible with either of the other two practices as you can either work your way through the Psalter, paraphrasing each one or letting your emotions guide you.

~ Choose a Psalm, either by working through the Psalter a Psalm at a time or by selecting a Psalm that speaks to the emotions of your life.

_____

[9] Malcolm Guite, *David's Crown: Sounding the Psalms* (Norwich: Canterbury Press, 2021).

~ Read it, noticing its language, tone and structure. Are there any images that particularly capture your attention or resonate with what you are experiencing or feeling?

~ Either write each line in your own words or write your own prayer based on the themes of the Psalm or the imagery that drew your attention.

~ Read what you have written aloud to yourself and to God.

Emotions & the Psalms

Most Psalms contain several emotions, and often they conflict. However, there are usually one or two dominant emotions. In her book *50 Ways to Pray*, Teresa Blythe includes this very helpful key for matching emotions with Psalms.[10] You may like to use it as a starting point when deciding which psalm you'd like to paraphrase or when trying to find a psalm that corresponds to your emotion.

Joy - Psalm 11, 18, 23, 27, 33, 84, 87, 103, 112, 122, 150
Peace - Psalm 23, 63, 103
Love - Psalm 33, 62, 99, 103, 104, 139, 145
Gratitude - Psalm 30, 32, 65, 75, 77, 103, 118, 136
Fear - Psalm 86, 130, 131
Anger or rage - Psalm 55, 58, 94
Persecution - Psalm 17, 26, 35, 69, 141
Distress - Psalm 29, 42, 44, 71, 88, 109, 113
Need for healing - Psalm 22, 38, 41
Need for justice - Psalm 26, 52, 114
Need for forgiveness - Psalm 39, 51

---

[10] Teresa A. Blythe, *50 Ways to Pray: Practices from Many Traditions and Times* (Nashville: Abingdon Press, 2006), 28.

LECTIO DIVINA

Lectio divina means "divine reading" and refers to an ancient approach to reading Scripture prayerfully. It is rooted in the belief that Scripture is enlivened by the Spirit, with power to speak to you where you are today. It originated in monastic communities, particularly the Benedictine and Carthusian orders, and is still practised by contemplative communities and individuals.

Lectio divina invites you to encounter God in Scripture in a profound and intimate way by teaching you how to open your ears, mind and heart to hear God's Word to you, today.

For more on *lectio divina*, I recommend Thelma Hall's *Too Deep for Words*[11] and Christine Valters Paintner's *Lectio Divina*[12], which expands the principles of *lectio divina* to include all the ways in which God speaks. The "Listen, Ask, Answer, Be" structure offered in the following practice is taken from Adam S. McHugh's *The Listening Life*.[13]

Practising

~ **Choose a text.** You can either work through a book of the Bible (the Gospels are a good place to start) or follow a lectionary (a book of assigned daily readings) or use a resource specifically aimed at *lectio divina* (for example Thelma Hall's, *Too Deep for Words*). Limit the number of verses you read; three or four is usually plenty.

~ **Listen.** Slowly read through the text at least two times. Read it aloud, if you can, and pause between sentences. Savour the words and pay attention to their tone and the emotion they carry

---

[11] Thelma Hall, *Too Deep for Words: Rediscovering Lectio Divina* (Mahwah: Paulist Press, 1988).
[12] Christine Valters Paintner, *Lectio Divina, the Sacred Art: Transforming Words and Images into Heart-Centered Prayer* (Woodstock, VT: Skylight Paths Publishing, 2011).
[13] Adam S. McHugh. *The Listening Life: Embracing Attentiveness in a World of Distraction* (Downers Grove, IL: IVP Books, 2015), 100-01.

as well as any pregnant silences in between words and sentences. Try to do this without judgement or analysis, gently observing your thoughts without getting entangled.

~ **Ask.** Read through the passage again, paying attention again to anything that stands out, or shimmers to you. Is there a word or phrase or image that offers itself to you? Does anything seem attractive or mysterious or important to you? If so, spend time with it. This is not the time for intellectual exercise or reading commentaries but for personal reflection. Reflect on it and why it seems important. You may like to dialogue with it; asking what it has to tell you. How does it speak to your life? Is there an invitation in it?

~ **Answer.** Read through the passage one more time. Speak to God inwardly or aloud about what you have read. Ask for the help you want; perhaps understanding or clarification, perhaps direction or forgiveness. Don't hold back. Be as honest as possible, knowing that God already knows you better than yourself and delights in relationship with you. Notice what happens.

~ **Be.** As your meditation deepens, let yourself receive what you have been offered. Accept what has or has not happened and settle back into God's presence beneath all experience and words. "Let the word you have heard sweep you up into God's embrace. Sit in silence, enjoying God and being with God without feeling pressure to speak or do anything. Let God sing love's song over you."[14] Linger here as long as you would like.

~ **End** with an Amen or a deep breath.

---

[14] Ibid., 101.

A note on praying with Bible
passages that you find challenging

Scripture isn't straightforward, and it isn't always comforting. Most people find reading certain passages challenging or distressing. Some passages have been weaponised by various factions of the church, some seem to reveal God to be unlike the God we have experienced, some stir up thoughts, feelings or memories that are painful. Although it is understandable to want to avoid these passages when praying with Scripture, it can also be deeply healing to approach these passages in the spirit of *lectio*, namely, by trying to be present to the passage as though for the first time, noticing and talking to God about what stands out or stirs within us, and then resting into God's tender embrace. If you pray this way with challenging passages, you may be surprised by what you notice or what bubbles to the surface during your meditation on it. Nevertheless, it's important to go gently so I recommend that you limit yourself to just a couple of lines and that you give yourself permission to stop at any time. You may also find it helpful to talk about your experience with a spiritual director or another trusted friend.

GOSPEL CONTEMPLATION

Gospel contemplation or the "prayer of Christ's memories" is another traditional method of prayerfully reading Scripture. It builds on a practice developed in the sixteenth century by Saint

Ignatius of Loyola who found that using his imagination when reading Scripture helped him to enter into the story and to receive deeper meaning from it. In gospel contemplation, the past becomes present through imagination and memory. The memory of the person praying becomes influenced by the memory of Jesus, now present to the person and this opens up the possibility of a profound encounter with Jesus and his teaching.

If you find it hard to connect with Scripture, if it feels remote or inaccessible, you may find this way of praying with Scripture helpful. By engaging your imagination as you read and pray, you short-circuit any impulse towards a bland or cold textual analysis and open yourself to a more holistic or soulful reading.

This practice develops a version of gospel contemplation offered by Chris Webb in his book *The Fire of the Word*, and direct quotes are his.[15] For Ignatius' teaching on gospel contemplation and the use of imagination in praying with Scripture see 'The Spiritual Exercises' in *Ignatius of Loyola, Spiritual Exercises and Selected Works*.[16]

Practising

~ Choose a passage from one of the Gospels. It's better to avoid a parable or a sermon passage, at least when you're beginning to pray in this way. Try selecting a passage in which Jesus' actions are at the centre, preferably one with colourful detail. Suggestions include Jesus' encounter with the Samaritan woman at the well (John 4:1-30), or with Nicodemus (John 3:1-21), or one of his miracles such as the calming of the storm (Matthew 8:23-27) or the feeding of the five thousand (Matthew 14:13-21).

---

[15] Chris Webb, *The Fire of the Word: Meeting God on Holy Ground* (Downers Grove, IL: IVP Books USA, 2011), 122-123.
[16] Ignatius of Loyola, *Spiritual Exercises and Selected Works* (Mahwah: Paulist Press, 1999).

~ Relax and settle yourself into God's presence. Acknowledge anything that is weighing on you. Is there an answer, gift or grace that you are seeking at this time? If so, name it.

~ Slowly read the passage. You can do this silently or aloud if circumstances allow and it is helpful to you. Pause as you let the scene sink into your imagination. Allow yourself permission to imagine the scene as clearly and vividly as you can. Let your imagination fill in the details and involve all your senses as you imagine sights, sounds, smells, flavours and textures.

~ Read the passage a second time, noticing details that you missed in the first reading. Again, pause and let your imagination develop the scene.

~ Read again, perhaps even a fourth or fifth time. Continue the pattern of reading and pausing to imagine until the gospel scene saturates your imagination.

~ As you allow the scene to unfold, see if you can observe the people involved and listen to their words as though you are part of the scene. Webb writes: "Allow yourself to be drawn into the scene as you imagine it. Place yourself in the shoes of one of the characters - a member of the crowd, an onlooker, a disciple, a questioner or a sick person lying before Christ."[17] If you feel drawn to do so, imagine yourself taking part in the activity in whatever way seems natural and appropriate. You might, for example, converse with them, accompany them or serve their needs.

~ As you engage in the scene present to you in imagination, notice your reactions. Webb asks "What feelings are stirred up as you

---

[17] Chris Webb, *The Fire of the Word: Meeting God on Holy Ground* (Downers Grove, IL: IVP Books USA, 2011), 122.

experience this gospel story? How do you want to respond to Jesus' questions and challenges?"[18]

~ Let these reactions guide you deeper into prayer. Speak to Christ "as one friend speaks to another." Allow yourself time to pause to listen for his response "trusting that Christ truly longs to speak with you."[19]

THE JESUS PRAYER

The Jesus prayer is a simple, heart-centred prayer that is both grounded in Scripture and rooted in the contemplative tradition. It reads, simply:

"Lord Jesus Christ, Son of God,
have mercy on me, a sinner."

This prayer joins together three Bible verses: the hymn of Paul's letter to the Philippians 2:6-11 (verse 11: "Jesus Christ is Lord"), the Annunciation of Luke 1:31-35 (verse 35: "Son of God"), and the parable of the Pharisee and the tax collector of Luke 18:9-14 (verse 13: "God, have mercy on me, a sinner."). It has been prayed throughout the Church's history, especially in the Eastern Orthodox Church in which it is intimately linked with hesychasm, the practice of still, contemplative prayer. The basis and foundation of this prayer is reverence for Jesus' name which is found repeatedly in

---

[18] Ibid., 122.
[19] Ibid., 123.

Scripture.[20] The following version of the practice is adapted from passages in *The Power of the Name* by Bishop Kallistos Ware.[21]

Practising

~ Sit comfortably and let your body be relaxed and inwardly alert. Close your eyes if you find this helpful to enter a sense of quietness. Pay attention to your breath, noticing how it slows you down as you become more still.

~ Join the Jesus Prayer with the rhythm of your breath. As you inhale, say aloud or silently, "Lord Jesus Christ, Son of God," and as you exhale you say, "have mercy on me, a sinner." You can also use an alternative formulation, for example, "Lord Jesus Christ, Son of God, share your risen life with me."

~ This prayer can be adjusted to fit your particular way of prayer. It can be shortened but should always include the name of Jesus. Some possibilities could be "Lord Jesus Christ, Son of God, have mercy on me," or "Lord Jesus Christ, have mercy," or "Lord, have mercy," or simply "Jesus."

~ If you find your mind wanders, don't judge yourself. Simply become aware again of the rhythm of your breath and join the Jesus Prayer to your breathing in a gentle way.

~ As you repeat the prayer, maintain an openness to receiving or hearing Jesus but let this be at a heart level of intent rather than by deliberately shaping any external image of Jesus. Trust, instead, that Jesus is at work in you, here and now.

---

[20] See Philippians 2:9-11, Acts 4:12, Luke 10:17, John 14:13, Romans 10:13, 1 Corinthians 6:11.
[21] Bishop Kallistos Ware, *The Power of the Name* (Oxford: SLG Press, 1974).

~ You can also repeat the Jesus Prayer "informally" by repeating the same prayer while going through your daily activities. This is a way of "praying without ceasing" (I Thessalonians 5:17) as your prayer becomes inextricably connected with your living and breathing in the world.

PRAYING SCRIPTURE AS A REFRAIN

The word refrain comes from the Latin word *refringere* which means "to repeat." To pray Scripture as a refrain means to pray a few words from Scripture repeatedly through the day. This continues the practice of *lectio divina* because it encourages deep and repeated meditation on a few lines of Scripture. Unlike the traditional practice of *lectio divina*, however, praying Scripture as a refrain can be practised throughout the day, rather than in one sitting. If you find yourself struggling to find time to pray with Scripture or are looking for a way to merge praying, reading Scripture and daily life, this practice may be particularly attractive or helpful.

Practising
~ Read a few verses of Scripture. You can either use an assigned reading for the day (perhaps using a lectionary or devotional) or choose a passage that resonates with your current situation or mood.

~ Read these verses again but more slowly, listening for the line or phrase that stands out in some way.

~ Repeat this line or phrase at regular times throughout the day.

~ To help you remember to pray this line or phrase you could try: setting a regular alarm or alert on your phone, associating your prayer with a routine prompt such as washing hands or drinking, writing it on your hand, writing it on a post-it, taking a photo and setting it as your screensaver for the day.

~ Before going to bed, you may like to end your day with a brief review of how that line or phrase has spoken to you today before releasing the words for the rest of sleep.

Praying with Nature

When I'm full of doubts or struggling with anxiety, it's usually nature that brings me back to God. The vastness of the sky, the beauty of a sunset, the intricacy of a butterfly's wings, the sound of birdsong all point beyond themselves to a mysterious and marvellous Creator. They also hold the paradoxical power to draw me out of myself while simultaneously re-grounding me. I'm reminded that I'm not an isolated individual but entwined with every natural phenomenon and living being in the fabric of nature; together we are held by creative love. It's an affirming yet deeply humbling experience. In those moments, I realise that I'm only whole when I recognise myself as part of a bigger whole whose every part opens onto God. It becomes impossible not to pray, and not just as myself but with all of nature.

I experienced the power of nature to open me to God in a particularly profound way during the Spring of 2020 when, like millions all over the globe, my family was subject to a stay-at-home order due to the Covid-19 pandemic. Life changed overnight. In some ways the changes were welcome: the restrictions meant that we suddenly had more time together as a family and some of our excessive busyness fell away. We had a richer appreciation for our health and tried to develop creative rhythms to balance schoolwork with play. We found joy in the simple, daily pleasure of being able to eat more meals together and became more tech savvy, discovering new ways to connect with friends and family. But other changes felt like losses. With everyone suddenly at home all day every day, we became acutely aware of the lack of personal space available in an open-plan apartment and found ourselves snapping at each other more than usual. We sighed as events on the calendar were cancelled and when family and friends couldn't visit, and we wrestled with our feeling of frustration when the lake front, beaches and state parks closed. We also had the additional complication of being in the middle of planning an international move from Chicago back to the UK. This entailed a long list of practical and logistical challenges but most painful for me was the thought of not being able to hug our friends goodbye.

In the midst of heaviness, the high point of each day was usually our walk around the neighbourhood. It was a relief to escape the apartment for an hour or so and, although we had nowhere in particular to go, these walks weren't aimless: it was spring and there was plenty to spot and enjoy in the sidewalk flower beds and the canopy of the tree-lined streets. Green shoots appeared out of the dirt, barren branches budded, ferns unfurled, flower stems grew tall and opened into colour. New life was everywhere and it was impossible not to be amazed. It was a welcome reminder that the natural world was carrying on, that our troubles were situated and held in the web of life.

These walks also had a sacramental quality. They imparted grace and strengthened my confidence that, even though it felt as though the rug had been pulled from under us, there was still cosmic order, purpose and meaning. I received every glimpse of flower bud or tightly curled frond as a divine gift; a reminder of the sacredness of creation and the honour of being both witness and participant. Even the broken, the dying, the torn or damaged seemed to speak of God as mysteriously present even in pain, struggle and loss.

I know I'm not alone in finding God in nature. So convinced were early Christian theologians that nature reveals God that it was common to speak of nature as a book "written" by God.

In the 4th century St Augustine wrote

> "Some people, in order to discover God, read books. But there is a great book: the very appearance of created things. Look above you! Look below you! Note it. Read it. God, whom you want to

discover, never wrote that book with ink. Instead, He set before your eyes the things that He had made. Can you ask for a louder voice than that? Why, heaven and earth shout to you: 'God made me!'"[1]

This understanding of nature as a book written by God continued throughout the Middle Ages. The book of nature was a book of revelation, not in competition or tension with Scripture but a second site of sacred encounter. To Protestants used to the principle of *sola Scriptura* (only Scripture) this may seem surprising, perhaps even shocking but the justification for thinking of nature as a book of revelation came from Scripture itself. In his letter to the early Christian community at Rome, St, Paul writes, "For since the creation of the world God's invisible qualities – his eternal power and divine nature – have been clearly understood from what has been made."[2] For St Paul, nature makes God known and being attentive to the world brings us closer to God.

Here, Paul echoes various Old Testament scriptures in which creation is affirmed as a place of revelation. For example, Psalm 19:1-4 reads:

"The heavens declare the glory of God;
  the skies proclaim the work of his hands.
Day after day they pour forth speech;
  night after night they reveal knowledge.
They have no speech, they use no words;
  no sound is heard from them.
Yet their voice goes out into all the earth,
  their words to the ends of the world."

Similarly, Wisdom of Solomon 13:5 tells us:

---

[1] St Augustine, "Sermon 126.6" in *The Essential Augustine,* trans. Vernon Bourke (Indianapolis: Hackett, 1974), 123.
[2] Romans 1:20

"For from the greatness and beauty of created things
comes a corresponding perception of their Creator."

And Job 12:7-19 commands:
"But ask the animals, and they will teach you, or the birds in the sky, and they will tell you; or speak to the earth, and it will teach you, or let the fish in the sea inform you. Which of all these does not know that the hand of the Lord has done this? In his hand is the life of every creature and the breath of all mankind."

Each of these passages presents nature as not just a neutral backdrop for spiritual experience but an opening onto divine encounter or, as the Dominican theologian Herbert McCabe puts it "a path toward God."[3]

This is not an anti-scientific approach to nature, and naming nature as a path to God doesn't preclude scientific investigation. While some may see science as flattening the mystery out of nature with the answer to every question we might have locked within each thing, ready to be laid bare and fully understood, many scientists discover the opposite: that in going deeper into the whys of nature, the more its complexity and wonder-fulness comes to the fore and the more they attune to God's presence.[4] Their example suggests that we don't need to choose between either a prayerful or a scientific approach to nature; both can deepen our desire to look at the natural world more closely and explore it

> Nature is not just a neutral backdrop for spiritual experience, but an opening onto divine encounter.

---

[3] Herbert McCabe, *God Matters* (London: Continuum, 1987), 7.
[4] For example, the biologist Francis Collins. See his book *Language of God: A Scientist Presents Evidence for Belief* (New York: Free Press, 2007).

further. Prayer can open onto science and science can become prayer. If nature is a path toward God, science can be a way to walk along it.

To pray with nature, then, means to allow ourselves to be fully present and attentive to it; to be captivated by it as we listen to what it has to tell us; to be willing to move along its path. Nature's invitation to respond prayerfully is offered at both a micro and a macro level, through both ocean and raindrop, mountaintop vista and DNA strand. It's also offered to us as both embodied and intellectual beings. The natural world invites us to gaze, listen, smell, touch, taste: to allow our senses to be spiritual guides as they bring us into the present and open us to receive what is offered. Nature also invites us to wonder, reflect and question. All this questioning is welcome and enfolded in a prayerful response. No question can take us away from God. As McCabe explains, all questioning about nature will bring us to the ultimate question "why is there something rather than nothing?" which is either a question we refuse to ask or a question whose answer is God.[5] For those who dare to ask, this question is transformative and in much the same way that allowing our senses to be spiritual guides can be transformative. It's as though we gain new ears to hear every sunset, ocean, forest and ant declare what Augustine could hear them shouting: "God made us!"

Praying with nature does not, however, mean simply thinking nice, spiritual things about nature or having a pleasant time outside and feeling connected to the Creator. As well as a willingness to be captivated by the natural world and to let that be a prayerful pathway, praying with nature means caring for nature. In other words, praying with nature is inextricably connected with ecological concern. One strengthens the other because the more we recognise nature as a sacred place of revelation and encounter, the more we'll

---

[5] Herbert McCabe, *God Matters* (London: Continuum, 1987), 7.

want to respect and tend to it. We won't want to own and possess, to control and dominate and the fact that this is exactly what human beings have done, will trouble us. Global warming, the hole in the ozone layer, deforestation and a steadily growing list of endangered species all highlight the ways in which we have treated the natural world as ours to use and abuse at will and a prayerful response means intentionally adjusting our lifestyles to bring healing to the natural world that reveals God. Learning a more sustainable way of life is not something extraneous to how we pray with nature but very much part of it: the rituals of recycling, reusing and refusing are all part of a rhythm of responding to a felt awareness of God's presence in nature.

This isn't to deny that Christianity has been in part (perhaps large part) to blame for the destruction of the natural world. As Lynn White, Jr argues, biblical passages have been used—both implicitly and explicitly—to justify an ownership-dominance approach to nature.[6] Junior points particularly to Genesis 1:28 in which God blesses Adam and Eve and tells them to "subdue" the earth and "rule over" living creatures.

It's easy to see how such language has been co-opted to support an aggressively anthropocentric approach to nature. But as is so often the case when it comes to sacred texts, context matters. Pope Francis has little time for Christians who would try to use Genesis 1.28 to support a destructive agenda and in his encyclical letter *Laudato Si*, stresses the importance of interpreting Genesis 1:28 in light of Genesis 2:8 in which Adam and Eve are instructed to till and keep the garden. As Pope Francis explains, tilling refers to cultivating, ploughing or working; and keeping means caring, protecting, overseeing and preserving. The relationship between human beings and nature in this passage isn't violent or aggressive but one of responsibility and concern. Set in this context, Genesis 1:28 isn't an instruction to dominate to the point of destruction but

---

[6] Lynn White, Jr, 'The Historical Roots of our Ecological Crisis' in *Science* (vol. 155, 10 March 1967), 1203-1207. Accessed on 4 April, 2022 at https://www.cmu.ca/faculty/gmatties/lynnwhiterootsofcrisis.pdf

to steward the land from which we gratefully receive. Of the "mutual responsibility" between human beings and nature, Pope Francis writes, "each community can take from the bounty of the earth whatever it needs for subsistence, but it also has the duty to protect the earth and to ensure its fruitfulness for coming generations."[7] For Pope Francis, sustainability is both biblical and spiritual.

When looking for a role model in how to pray with nature, there is, perhaps, no better example than Pope Francis's namesake, the 13th century Italian St Francis of Assisi. Now recognised by the Roman Catholic Church as the patron saint of ecology, St Francis fully embodied the caring and respectful approach to the natural world which Pope Francis advocates in *Laudato Si*.

St Francis is often depicted surrounded by birds and other animals, a reference to the many stories about him contained within his hagiographies. In these biographies we're told that St Francis preached to birds, chastened and forgave a wolf that had been terrorising a local community, released rabbits from traps and freed fish caught in nets, warning them not to get caught again. In all these stories, St Francis addresses the animals as brothers and sisters, expressing his deep awareness of the interconnectedness of all living beings.

As with many of the saints, it's hard to separate fact from fiction, the man from the legend, but regardless of the precise historicity of these stories, the picture that emerges is of a man who was deeply compassionate and aware of the sacred bonds between all creatures. This compassion wasn't a sentimental anthropomorphising of nature but was rooted in his deep love of Christ whom he recognised as present in all things. This was also the source of his compassion for human beings, in particular for the vulnerable, the poor, the sick and the dying. Sometimes attention to nature is pitted against attention to human beings but St Francis shows that truly deep concern for one necessarily entails deep concern for the other. As Pope Francis writes: "[Saint Francis] shows us just how inseparable

---

[7] Pope Francis, *Praise be to You - Laudato Si': On Care for Our Common Home* (San Francisco: Ignatius Press, 2015), 67.

71

the bond is between concern for nature, justice for the poor, commitment to society, and interior peace."[8]

Keeping St Francis' example at the forefront of my mind has been helpful when learning to playfully pray with nature. St Francis' approach to nature encourages me to be open to receiving every living being and natural phenomenon as teacher and spiritual guide. All are creatures and all reveal something of the invisible, mysterious Creator. This isn't pantheism—the belief that God is contained by nature – but an iconic understanding of creation in which all things, in their very being, *participate* in God and are windows through which we glimpse God. We honour both creation and God when we allow our wonder and praise to flow from creature to Creator. This draws us deeper into relationship with both God and the created world because, when we recognise that each part of creation reveals God, we gain a stronger sense of the connection between ourselves and the fabric of creation: we are all held lovingly by the same transcendent One.

> *...we can all receive the natural world as a cathedral, a place of prayer and retreat.*

Allowing St Francis' example to guide me, has also helped me to be less prescriptive about how I approach praying in and with nature. I don't need to have an agenda or even expectations. It is enough simply to step outdoors and let nature unwind whatever has become too tightly wound within me. Like St Francis, we can all receive the natural world as a cathedral, a place of prayer and retreat. We don't need to wait for a particular vista or the right weather but can open ourselves to receive all our time in nature as a place of encounter with God.

St Francis also encourages me to prayerfully affirm my kinship, not only with other human beings but with all of nature. This means

[8] Ibid., 10.

recognising that the skies and sun and trees and animals and elements are not brute facts of my environment but fellow creatures, worthy not only of admiration and wonder but also of attention and care. Like St Francis, I am learning to honour them as my brothers and sisters.

In the following pages you will find a selection of practices to help you to begin to pray with and through nature. They are offered lightly, and while I hope there may be something here to pique your interest, I also hope you will feel inspired to explore your own unique way to pray with the natural world that surrounds you. Begin with whatever creature or natural phenomenon provokes your curiosity or elicits wonder and let it be your guide.

For reflection

When have you experienced God or God's presence in nature?

I am not an isolated individual but entwined with every living thing in the fabric of nature and we are all held by the Creator who sustains us in existence. How do you feel about this statement? Do you tend to think of yourself as isolated or entwined?

What attracts you to, or hinders you from, spending time in nature?

WONDER WALK

Most religious traditions include a form of nature or walking meditation. Jesus models this in the Gospels by choosing to teach outside, using the sensual natural world as both the backdrop and entry way to his message. "Look at the lilies..." he says to those who listen, both then and now.[9]

While you may already spend at least some portion of your day outside, it's easy to be distracted and it can be a struggle to be present to our surroundings. A wonder walk invites you to turn your time outside into an intentional spiritual practice that cultivates openness, curiosity and wonder. This practice is grounded in the belief that all of nature is saturated with God's presence and that becoming present to your natural surroundings will also return you to God's presence. There is no aim in particular, simply a deepening of your willingness to notice and receive from your natural surroundings as you listen for God's invitation to you.

Practising

~ Begin by inwardly affirming your intention to see anew the world present all around you.

~ Take a slow walk outside alone or with someone else. If you have company, choose not to talk to each other for a while so that you can be more aware of everything else around you. You can take a walk in your home, garden, neighbourhood or out in the mountains, by the seaside, or along a riverfront. You might like to consider walking barefoot so you can more intimately feel your connection with your surroundings.

~ Move slowly, noticing the sensations in your body, for example: discomfort, surprise, challenge, pleasure, ease. Take in your

---

[9] Luke 12:27.

surroundings with a soft, receptive gaze. What do you see? What do you hear? What can you smell? Is there anything to touch or taste? Savour your surroundings through your senses.

~ Allow your attention to rest wherever you are led. Sink into your awareness, breathing deeply as you open yourself to receive it more fully.

~ Continue to walk and to be present and open to what is around, beneath, above and within you. Be awake to any invitations there may be for you and be open to how these might arrive.

~ End by bowing in gratitude for your body, for the world surrounding you and, in particular, for whatever particularly drew your attention.

~ Afterwards, you may like to reflect. Pay attention to your body as well as your feelings and thoughts as you ask yourself these questions:

What was it like to become aware, or more intensely aware of my surroundings?

What did I notice, either around me or within me?

How am I being invited to respond?

A Wonder Walk Prayer

This wonder walk can be adapted in several ways. One suggestion is to walk with the intention of noticing beauty. To begin this walk, you may like to slowly read or recite this Navajo prayer.[10]

In beauty I walk
With beauty before me I walk
With beauty behind me I walk
With beauty above me I walk
With beauty around me I walk
It has become beauty again
It has become beauty again
It has become beauty again
It has become beauty again

As you walk, ask yourself "where is beauty?" and at the end bow to the beauty around you and the beauty that will follow you wherever you go.

PRAYING WITH THE ELEMENTS

This prayer builds on the "Canticle of the Sun", a prayer written by St Francis of Assisi in the thirteenth century. St Francis was deeply aware of God's presence in all of creation and spoke of the elements and animals as "brothers" and "sisters" joining in praise of a shared Creator God. It is also deeply aligned with Celtic

---

[10] Author unknown. A longer version of this prayer is available at https://talking-feather.com/home/walk-in-beauty-prayer-from-navajo-blessing/ (accessed 4 April, 2022). The prayer is entitled "Walking in Beauty" and it is included as the closing prayer from the Navajo Way Blessing Ceremony.

Christianity in which nature is honoured as sacred space and the elements coexist with each other and with all creatures. For more on St Francis, see Richard Rohr's *Eager to Love* and for more on the sacred significance of the elements in Celtic Christianity, see *The Four Elements* by John O'Donohue. The excerpts quoted below are from "The Canticle of the Sun".[11]

Practising

~ Gather together a bowl, a glass or jug of water and a candle. You will use each of these in turn.

~ Begin with a moment of silence to centre yourself and become present to this moment and open yourself to acknowledging and receiving God's blessing through the elements.

Air

~ Say or read:

> *"Praised be You, my Lord,*
> *through Brothers Wind and Air,*
> *And fair and stormy, all weather's moods,*
> *by which You cherish all that You have made."*

~ Breathe the air in deeply.

~ Reflect on the blessing of air. We marvel at the power of air to bring change. Through gales and tornadoes and gentle breezes, wind stirs, unsettles and reveals. Air brings music: rustling, sighing, howling. Air cools us on a hot day, brings chill in winter.

---

[11] In this practice, I have adapted and excerpted a longer version of this prayer which may be found at https://www.catholic.org/prayers/prayer.php?p=3188 (accessed 4 April, 2022).

Air carries scents and evokes memory. Air fills our lungs with the breath of life.

~ When or how have air and wind blessed you? Try to recall particular experiences. In these moments, how were wind and air brothers to you? What might these moments have to tell you about God?

~ Thank God for the gift of wind.

Water

~ Say or read:

> *"Praised be You, my Lord,*
> *through Sister Water,*
> *So useful, humble, precious and pure."*

~ Pour water into a bowl. Touch or drink the water.

~ Reflect on the blessing of water. Water shapes earth's canyons and coastlines. It surrounded us with warmth and safety in our mother's womb and continues to sustain us in life. Water nourishes the earth and brings crops to fruition. Water refreshes us and cleanses us. Water awes us with beauty in waterfalls, lakes, oceans, mists and when frozen in ice and snow.

~ When or how has water been a sister to you? Recall a particular experience and reflect on what it might have to teach you: about water, about yourself, about God.

~ Thank God for the blessing of sister water.

Fire

~ Say or read:

> *"Praised be You, my Lord,*
> *through Brother Fire,*
> *through whom You light the night*
> *and he is beautiful and playful*
> *and robust and strong."*

~ Light a candle. Watch the flame flicker and feel its warmth.

~ Reflect on the gift of brother fire. Fire brings light and illumination and shows us the way to walk. Fire purifies, burning away what is dried and dead and making way for fresh, new growth. Fire comforts and warms us. Fire dazzles us and dances for us.

~ How or when has fire been a blessing for you? What have been your experiences of fire? What emotions or images do you associate with fire? In what way might fire be your brother? How might you join fire in praising God?

~ Thank God for the gift of brother fire.

Earth

~ Say or read:

> *"Praised be You, my Lord,*
> *through our Sister, Mother Earth*
> *who sustains and governs us,*
> *producing varied fruits*
> *with coloured flowers and herbs."*

~ Take your shoes off and feel the connection with the ground.

~ Reflect on the blessing of Mother Earth. Green valleys; lush pastures; sandy deserts; rooted woodlands: the contours and textures of earth are innumerable. The abundance of earth's harvests sustains our life. She shapes us and forms us from the very elements of herself. From deep within her molten core, she reshapes, reforms and renews herself. Earth grounds us and makes firm our steps and enfolds us when the journey is complete.

~ For which of Earth's many corners are you most thankful? Recall a place where you have felt grounded and secure. How might thinking of this place as a mother to you shape your thinking of earth, yourself and God?

~ Thank God for the gift of Mother Earth.

To close:

~ Say or read:

> *"Most High, all-powerful, all-good Lord,*
> *All praise is Yours, all glory,*
> *all honour and all blessings.*
> *Praised be You, my Lord,*
> *with all Your creatures."*

~ Offer all your thanks and praise to God who creates not out of need but love. Picture yourself gathered with all the elements, surrendered to God in wonder and praise.

ASKING ANOTHER LIVING CREATURE TO TEACH YOU

While the Genesis account of creation names only human beings as made in the image of God, the Bible repeatedly affirms that every living being and natural phenomenon originates in God's joyful creativity and reveals God in its own unique way. As Thomas Aquinas explains, all creatures bear "some kind of likeness to God"; in humans this likeness is found through the likeness of "image" and in other creatures through the likeness of "trace".[12] This practice offers you a way to honour the trace of God that is to be found in every creature, encouraging you to be open to being surprised by what it may have to reveal to you.

Practising

~ Begin by reading the following passages:

> "But ask the animals, and they will teach you, or the birds in the sky, and they will tell you; or speak to the earth, and it will teach you, or let the fish in the sea inform you. Which of all these does not know that the hand of the Lord has done this? In his hand is the life of every creature and the breath of all mankind." Job 12:7-10

> "Apprehend God in all things, for God is in all things. Every creature is full of God and is a book about God. Every creature is a word of God. If I spent enough time with the tiniest creature – even a caterpillar –I would

---

[12] "While in all creatures there is some kind of likeness to God, in the rational creature alone we find a likeness of 'image'... whereas in other creatures we find a likeness by way of a 'trace'" *Summa Theologica* I.93.6 resp (London: Washborne, 1911). Bonaventure also uses this distinction between image and vestige in *Breviloquium* II.12.1.

never have to prepare a sermon, so full of God is every creature." Meister Eckhart[13]

~ Choose one animal, bird or fish. It could be a pet, or one you have seen on a walk, or one that has captured your imagination in the past. If you can't see it in the flesh, try to find a picture or some video footage.

~ Look at it closely. What do you see? Notice its form, its texture, its patterns and colour. If you are attending to a living thing rather than to a picture, also notice how it moves, what sounds it makes and how it makes them and follow it as it moves. Focus your effort on staying present to it and let it guide your attention.

~ Inwardly ask God what it has to teach you, trusting that all creatures have something to tell us about our shared Creator. If nothing comes to you immediately, keep returning to the image or hold it in your mind during the day.

~ Offer your thanks to God, the Creator, for this being and for its wisdom.

CREATING A NATURE TABLE
TO CELEBRATE THE SEASONS

Celtic spirituality gives a privileged place to engagement with the seasons and encourages a more cyclical rhythm to the year. The liturgical year, with its seasons of Advent, Christmas, Epiphany,

---

[13] Cited in *Earth Prayers: 365 Prayers, Poems, and Invocations from Around the World*, eds. Elizabeth Roberts and Elias Amidon (San Francisco: HarperOne, 2009), 251.

Lent, Easter and Pentecost builds on a natural rhythm of ebb and flow through the seasons, and there need not be a tension between celebrating the liturgical and natural rhythms of the year.

One way to engage prayerfully with the seasons is by creating an altar somewhere in your home that is a reminder of the sacred presence in this current season.

Practising

~ Decide where your nature table will live. Suggestions include a small table, a shelf, or even a windowsill.

~ In the centre, place a cross or other symbol of God's presence. This will remain in place through the seasons.

~ Around it, place objects or photographs or fabric that remind you of this particular season. You can also add items that remind you of the current liturgical season, for example, Advent, Christmas, Epiphany, Lent, Easter, Pentecost.

~ Each day offer a prayer or quiet moment of gratitude for this season and ask for your eyes to be opened to see God's presence all about you.

~ To mark the ending of one season and the beginning of another, you may like to read Psalm 104, a Psalm of praise that celebrates how God is revealed through and intimately present to creation.

PRAYING THE WEATHER

Most of us are affected by the weather, at least to some degree. Our spirits tend to be raised by blue sky and sunlight and to fall on a grey, gloomy day. Sometimes we think this is something to overcome and a sign of weakness to be so easily swayed but perhaps it's actually a natural consequence of being entwined with creation. This practice invites you to embrace the weather as offering you an opportunity to become more present, both to your surroundings and to your inner life.

Practising

~ If you are able, go outside. If not, find a window you can sit or stand beside.

~ Remind yourself of God's presence with you and within all of creation. You may like to do this with words or with a bodily gesture, for example by upturning your palms.

~ Notice the weather. Use your senses to help you. What temperature is the air? How does it feel against your skin? Is there a sound? A scent? A flavour?

~ How is the weather affecting your surroundings? Is there movement? Are there sounds? Are things being concealed or revealed, enhanced or destroyed?

~ How is the weather affecting you? How does your body respond? Is there an emotional response? Does it remind you of something or someone?

~ Gather all these noticings and offer them to God, either with words or through breathing the air slowly and deeply.

RETREATING TO A SIT SPOT

All of creation participates in, reveals and offers a pathway towards God, if only we have eyes to see. There are, however, some places where we may, mysteriously, become particularly aware of God's presence. In Celtic Christianity these are referred to as "thin" places, where the distinction between earth and heaven seems to dissolve. This practice will help you to become aware of where these are and encourage you to commit to spending regular time there as part of a prayerful life.

Practising

~ Take some time to reflect on where in your home, garden or neighbourhood you find it easiest to pray. Ask yourself:

> *Where am I most aware of God's presence with me, within me, or in creation?*

> *Where do I notice myself breathing more deeply or moving more slowly?*

> *Where do I tend to go for refreshment when I am feeling tired or overwhelmed?*

> *Where do I feel safe to be vulnerable?*

~ Claim this spot as a thin place by placing something in that place as a symbol and reminder of its significance to you. If it is in your home you could put up a picture or photograph that opens you to prayer. You may also want to leave a Bible or a journal in that place or anything else that nourishes prayer. If your thin place is in your garden or neighbourhood consider making a cairn (see below) as a marker of it as a significant place for you.

~ Return to this spot as regularly as you can, as part of your spiritual practice. Allow yourself to linger there, letting it unwind whatever is binding you and showing you how to open yourself in prayer, in whatever is authentic for you.

Cairns

A cairn is a pile of stones that is carefully placed to indicate either a pathway or a significant site. To create one, simply collect a few stones and place them in or around your sit spot. Don't overthink how you arrange them, let your intuition guide you. You may also wish to draw words or shapes in the sand or dirt with a twig. These will eventually be washed away but the memory of creating them and of the significance of this place for you will remain.

RECYCLING PRAYER

Choosing to reuse or recycle can become an intentional spiritual practice by bringing awareness to the way in which it contributes to our shared responsibility to tend and steward the earth and her resources. There are several ways you could bring this awareness to your habits of reusing or recycling. The following are suggestions for how you might make each small act of recycling or reusing into a prayerful moment.

Practising

~ At the point at which you recognise you are making a choice to recycle or reuse, consider offering one of the following, or similar:

> **An affirmation of intent.** For example: "I care for the earth", or "I honour mother nature."

> **A brief silent or spoken prayer.** For example: "The earth is yours", or "Thank you."

> **A word of blessing for the earth.** For example: "May you flourish."

~ Pause briefly to bring attention to your physical movement of choosing to reuse or recycle rather than replace or discard.

Praying with Our Intellects

Childhood images of God linger. Sometimes these images are rich and nourish us well beyond childhood. Others need to be released in order to allow growth. This process of release is often much more difficult than we may initially think. It's hard, if not impossible, to simply "switch off" an image. Even when we think we have outgrown them, they continue to lurk and often reveal themselves subtly in our approach to prayer. As a spiritual director, I've noticed that the common childhood image of God as a distant, observant man in heaven is one which shows up frequently and tends to make prayer feel either irrelevant or like a performance.

Wanting to instil healthy images of God that will open up a relationship, I've tried to be careful about how I present God to my children. God is love, God is mysterious, God is within, God is all around, God is parent, God is friend. I try to vary the images I use and draw on Scripture to help. Rachel Held Evans' little book *What Is God Like?* has also been a great resource. And yet, as well intentioned as this has been, I think I have sometimes caused more issues than I have resolved, albeit with humorous effect.

"God is with you always, close to you, in your heart."

"So, if you cut me open, you'll find God?"

"Well, not exactly."

"Why do you say that God is in my heart then?"

"It's my way of saying that God is right in the middle of what makes you, you."

"Oh, so God's not *in* my heart, God is *next to* my heart."

Trying to explain metaphors to children is tricky but I wonder how many adult Christians are also confused by what is meant by "heart". The word occurs frequently in Scripture and is used regularly in church settings but often without explanation. As is usually the case, it's easier to say what the metaphorical heart is not. It isn't the physical muscle, it isn't the source of sentimental feelings, it isn't even a metaphor for the seat of emotions. Rather, it is the symbolic, yet real centre of a person. It is the inmost self: the place where all our faculties converge and where spiritual struggle occurs. The heart is mysterious and deep, opening onto God's own presence. The state of one's heart reveals the truth of oneself with the hard of heart being those who resist the movement of love and the faithful of heart being those who rest in God's loving gaze.

In spirituality, the heart is often contrasted with the head. As with heart, "head" is intended not so much as a physical locator as a metaphor for the place of thinking that we refer to as our intellect. For many people, the spiritual journey is one from head to heart – from thinking about God and giving mental assent to statements of belief, to becoming caught in the flow of God's love. Such a journey takes time and effort. In his article 'Loving God with Heart and Mind,' Alister McGrath recalls his friend Donald Coggan's remark that "The journey from head to heart is one of the longest and most difficult that we know."[1]

McGrath goes on to talk about his journey from an academic faith to one more heart centred. "My experience," writes McGrath, "is that we need to *go deeper*, rather than just *know more*."[2] While he emphasises the importance of understanding the tenets of faith, he also stresses that remaining at the level of knowledge results in a faith that is dry and cerebral. For our faith to flourish it must descend from our heads to our hearts: the words which we hear and learn must take root in our hidden centre.

> For our faith to flourish it must descend from our heads to our hearts.

McGrath is not alone in his experiences or convictions. In *The Way of the Heart*, Henri Nouwen is critical of the Western church for placing so much focus on the intellect and neglecting the heart. Such an approach turns God into a problem to be solved, prayer into

---

[1] Alister McGrath, 'Loving God with Heart and Mind' in *Knowing and Doing* (Winter 2002), 1.
[2] Ibid., 2.

another exhausting intellectual activity, and makes it hard for us to listen and respond to God with our whole selves. "The crisis of our prayer life," writes Nouwen, "is that our mind may be filled with ideas of God while our heart remains far from him. Real prayer comes from the heart."[3]

As an antidote, Nouwen advocates what he refers to as "the way of the heart"—a way of praying that builds on the practices of the desert fathers and mothers of the third and fourth centuries and is less grasping, less about doing and thinking, and more about surrendering to being with God in love.

I am grateful to those such as McGrath and Nouwen who act as guides along the journey from head to heart. My own journey from detached thinking about God to intimate encounter with God has been helped along by their example and writings. Releasing my impulse to grasp God intellectually and allowing myself to experience God more intuitively has strengthened my faith. I've discovered that God longs to meet me in my body, in my imagination, in the daily events of my life. I've become more open to experiencing what I don't yet understand. And yet I still long to understand, to engage my intellectual faculties in my relationship with God. As I continue to study theology and think about God, I've also found myself longing for guides to help me better integrate my theological reflection into my prayer life. Without such guides I feel myself in danger of opposing thinking to praying, of keeping my study of God separate from praying to God, of replacing head with heart, rather than seeing head as enfolded within heart.

Thankfully, this longing for a guide has been answered, and repeatedly. Through study and conversation, I have encountered many theologians who have both articulated and modelled a prayerful synthesis of head and heart. One particularly helpful guide

---

[3] Henri Nouwen, *The Way of the Heart: Connecting with God Through Prayer, Wisdom and Silence* (New York: Ballantine, 1983), 71.

has been the 13th century Dominican Saint, Thomas Aquinas—although, admittedly, this might not be clear from a cursory look at his writings. On the surface, these appear to give strong priority to head over heart. For one thing, his style of writing seems cold and austere, almost impenetrable to anyone unacquainted with Aristotelian philosophy or thirteenth century scholasticism. For another, he understands prayer to be an intellectual activity. This applies to both petitionary prayer (in which we make requests of God) and contemplation (in which our intellect gazes on God without distractions).[4]

Closer study of his writings, however, makes it clear that Aquinas is by no means all head and no heart. While he does strongly favour the intellect, he doesn't understand it to be a faculty distinct from the heart or from love. For Aquinas, love and intellect go together in a life of prayer because it's love that moves our spoken prayers and allows us to unveil our minds before God.[5] It's only because we love God that we turn our minds to God in prayer. This turning to God through spoken prayer begins a process of opening to God that finds its truest expression in contemplation, an activity of both love and intellect. Contemplation is not a cold disinterested looking at God but a pleasurable and loving gazing upon God.[6] In contemplation, we move beyond words and spoken prayers to a more intimate way of being with God in love: a love that fuses our hearts with our minds.

Aquinas' lived example underlines his value as a guide into the integration of head and heart through prayer. Prayer didn't simply bookend Aquinas' study but was an integral part of the process. At his canonisation proceedings, his friend Brother Reginald of Piperno recounted that "when perplexed by a difficulty he would kneel and pray and then, on returning to his writing and dictation,

---

[4] See Thomas Aquinas, *Summa Theologica* (hereafter *ST*), II-II, q.83, a1 and II-II, q180, al.
[5] See *ST*, II-II, q.83, a1, r2.
[6] See *ST* II-II, 1.180, a7.

he was accustomed to find that his thought had become so clear that it seemed to show him inwardly, as in a book, the words he needed."[7]

And yet it would be a mischaracterisation to say that Aquinas used prayer as a means to an end of completing study. Rather, prayer and study combined in a movement closer to God, to contemplation and enjoyment of God with mind and heart. That his study was directed towards prayer, instead of prayer towards study, can be seen by the fact that his longest piece of work (*Summa Theologica*) was deliberately left unfinished following a mystical experience in prayer. The details of this experience remain mysterious, but its transformative power is clear from Aquinas' words to Brother Reginald: "All that I have written seems to me nothing but straw...compared to what I have seen and what has been revealed to me."[8]

After this experience Aquinas was noticeably different. He largely gave up writing and became quieter. This surprised and confused those around him, some of whom thought he must have become unwell. But as his biographers over the centuries have stressed, Aquinas' silence was not due to a loss of knowledge but to an excess. He had moved to a place beyond the reach of words and his silence was a reverent response. Nothing more was needed.

...when we invite God into our thinking, our thinking is already prayer.

That Aquinas was willing to move into this silence indicates that his earlier study had been aimed at the pursuit of intimacy *with* God through faith and reason rather than a mastery of knowledge *about* God.

Following Aquinas' lead, we don't need to separate our thinking from our praying. We can address our thinking to God and affirm that all our thinking, insofar as it is aimed at the understanding of what is true, is aimed at contemplation: the vision of God who is

[7] Bernard Gui, *The Life of St Thomas Aquinas*, ed. Kenelm Foster (Longmans: London, 1959), 36.
[8] As cited by James A. Weisheipl in *Friar Thomas D'Aquino: His Life, Thought and Work* (New York: Doubleday, 1974), 321-22.

Truth. We are invited to share our minds with God and to see head and heart as integrated in our response to God. Thinking as prayer is not a linear process in which thinking leads to insights leads to prayer. Rather, when we invite God into our thinking, our thinking is already prayer. We open our minds to God, offering our thoughts and our desire to know more and wait expectantly for illumination, not so that we may possessively grasp things, but so we will be led deeper into prayer and the enjoyment of the marvellous mystery of God. Like Aquinas, we learn to "kneel down in spirit...before the mystery."[9]

Aquinas' writings and pattern of living make it unsurprising that he is the patron saint of people engaged in a long list of educational and theological activities, including theologians, philosophers, academics and students. But although he offers us strong encouragement to pray with our intellects, it's important to emphasise that he stands in the company of a host of other pre-modern writers who share his conviction that prayer and study go hand in hand. Indeed, this belief is often clearer in their writings than in Aquinas'. Whereas Aquinas' works are mainly structured in a formalised way echoing the style of debate used in the universities of his day, many other pre-modern theologians wrote their theology *as* prayer with all their intellectual wrestling offered to God.

St Augustine's *Confessions*, perhaps the best known pre-modern Christian spiritual work, is a lovely example of intellectual wrestling offered as prayer. In this text, whenever Augustine is wondering about something, he addresses it to God. As he prays his thoughts, questions and doubts, he either reaches insights or finds the courage to stay in the uncertainty or is able to release the question altogether. All is done in response to a loving God. For example, he writes:

---

[9] Paul Murray, *Aquinas at Prayer: The Bible, Mysticism and Poetry* (London: Bloomsbury, 2013), 10.

"O Lord, since you are outside time in eternity, are you unaware of the things that I tell you? Or do you see in time the things that occur in it? If I see them, why do I lay this lengthy record before you? Certainly it is not through me that you first hear of these things. But by setting them down I fire my own heart and the hearts of my readers with love of you, so that we all may ask: can any praise be worthy of the Lord's majesty? I have said before, and I shall say again, that I write this book for love of your love."[10]

Another of the pre-modern greats, St Anselm, also offers his thoughts to God as prayer. Anselm, best known for his so-called "ontological argument" for the existence of God, is sometimes characterised as a naïve rationalist who believed God could be grasped. And yet, the inadequacy of this view is apparent to anyone who actually reads his argument in context. Doing so makes it clear that Anselm's objective is not to prove God exists as though God were an object of study, subordinate to rational enquiry, but rather to understand better the One whom he already knows and loves. "Well then, Lord," Anselm writes, "You who give understanding to faith, grant me that I may understand, as much as you see fit, that you exist as we believe you to exist, and that you are what we believe you to be."[11]

For both Augustine and Anselm, theology is not just words *about* God, but words addressed *to* God. Although there are differences in the focus and conclusions of their theological study, they both agree that reasoning is meant to happen in the context of faith. Faith is itself a way of knowing that goes ahead of reason and opens up a space in which it can work. And, ultimately, reason falls back into the encompassing presence of faith as we reach the limits of our understanding. Faith and reason are not opposed: faith anchors and

---

[10] Augustine, *Confessions* (London: Penguin, 1961), 253.
[11] Anselm, 'Proslogion' in *Anselm of Canterbury: The Major Works*, eds. Davies, Brian and Evans (Oxford: OUP, 1998), 87.

completes reason. For these men of faith and reason, prayer does not come after thinking but underwrites it.

Today's academic theology might appear to have been written outside the realm of prayer but there are still many with personal faith who don't demarcate their life of study from their life of prayer. One of my academic theologian friends lights a candle when he reads texts he believes are particularly truthful and worthy of attention. In addition to the many theologians of faith working within universities and other institutions, the Dominican order are strong advocates of study as prayer and of praying as a practice that engages intellect as well as heart and body. Following Aquinas' example, Dominicans "display a thirst for Truth and an openness to seek it wherever and from whomever it may be found; [they] are beggars of Truth."[12]

Faith and reason are not opposed: faith anchors and completes reason.

Such beggars of truth are also to be found in other areas of academic study. Alister McGrath, with whom we began this chapter, is a good example of someone for whom faith and reason are married together in pursuit of a closer relationship with God who is both Love and Truth. In his article 'Breaking the Science-Atheism Bond' he writes:

> "My Christian faith brings me a deepened appreciation of the natural sciences...Why does faith bring this intellectual enthusiasm and satisfaction? In the words of another academic from Belfast who found faith at Oxford University: 'I believe in Christianity as I believe that the Sun has risen-not only because I see

[12] See the article 'Dominican Contemplation: Prayer and Study in order to Preach' at www.english.op.org.

it, but because by it, I see everything else.' [C. S.] Lewis conceives God in a manner that illuminates the great riddles and enigmas of life, including how and why it is that we can make sense of the universe at all. His conception offers me an understanding of my own place in the greater scheme of things, and at the same time provides an intellectual Archimedean point from which I can make sense of the world around me. Above all, it sustains my sense of awe at the wonders of nature, and the greater wonders to which they point."[13]

McGrath doesn't explicitly talk about his study as prayer but his and Lewis' understanding of God as the sunlight through which all is seen is the foundation of a prayerful approach to study, not only of theology but of all things including the natural world. Today, science and faith are often pitted against each other but McGrath's example suggests that believing in God doesn't eliminate our need to study; rather, it intensifies our desire to wonder, explore and understand. For scientists of faith, scientific enquiry and prayer are not opposed. To the contrary, because God is the source and goal of all things, science already has a theological flavour: to learn about God's creatures is also to learn something about God.

This chapter contains several suggestions to help to begin to integrate head with heart, to pray with your intellect. You will find practices to help you integrate head with body, to study prayerfully and to use wonder as a gateway to intellectual prayer. These practices don't require a high IQ or a background in academia. Those who tend to identify with their intellects or thinking more than their emotions or bodies will likely find these practices

---

[13] Alistair McGrath, 'Breaking the Science-Atheism Bond' in *Science and Spirit Magazine*, reprinted at https://www.beliefnet.com/news/science-religion/2005/08/breaking-the-science-atheism-bond.aspx

appealing and may already naturally pray in these ways, but my hope is that they will be accessible and engaging for all, even for those who don't tend to regard themselves as thinkers. In addition to our bodies, imaginations, memories and creativity (among other things), we have all been gifted our measure of intellect and we are welcome and encouraged to use all in our response to God.

For reflection

Where are you on the journey from head to heart?

Do you find that you are able to address your thought processes to God?

Do you sometimes think about God as a problem to be solved?

How do faith and reason relate in your life?

Have you experienced study as prayer?

A BLESSING FOR THE INTEGRATION
OF BODY, INTELLECT AND HEART

In Judeo-Christian theology, the heart is not a sentimental metaphor for the site of your emotions but refers to your hidden centre, where all your faculties converge, including intellect, will and imagination as well as your emotions. The state of your heart reveals the truth about you and the spiritual life is concerned with the heart-centred transformation. Many spiritual writers talk about the importance of "descending from the head to the heart" by which they mean intentionally moving from a detached or surface level awareness to a deeper, more soulful way of being present. In order for this to happen, you have to allow your physical experiences and intellectual understanding to touch you at your deepest level.

Even if you are open to this process, it can be hard to know how to begin. One way is through blessing your faculties and drawing them towards your centre as you affirm that your body, intellect and heart have been created by the same God and are meant to be integrated into your journey home to God. The particular wording is not as important as your intention to respectfully acknowledge the significance of each aspect of your being so feel free to adapt it. You may also like to bless other faculties important to you in your spiritual life and journey.

Practising

~ With hands outstretched:

> *God, I thank you for my body. For my breath, for my senses, for my portion of strength, for my flesh, skin and bone – however they may be marked - for the ability to experience the seasons and the physical world. Bless my movements, my seeing, hearing, smelling, touching, tasting. May I experience you in and through your physical creation.*

~ With hands on head:

> *God, I thank you for my intellect. For thoughts and ideas, for curiosity, for my capacity – whatever it may be – to learn and understand. Bless my mind, guide my thoughts and questions. May I seek you in and through my thinking.*

~ With hands on heart:

> *God, I thank you for my heart. The centre of my being, where all my faculties converge - my intellect, my emotions, my imagination, my will. Bless my hidden centre. May every seed of encounter with you through body and mind descend to my heart, take root and grow.*

~ You can then move to praying with just the gestures – arms out, hands on head, hands on heart. Allow the movements to guide your body and intellect towards your centre.

PRAYING TO BEGIN A PERIOD OF STUDY

How we begin is important. A good beginning settles and steadies us, opening up a space in which to move forwards. If you are attracted by the idea of offering study as prayer, you might like to begin with a prayerful ritual or practice. This may help you to approach your study in a soulful or heart-centred way by acknowledging that your thirst for knowledge is a thirst for wisdom that is accessible and yet, in its completeness, mysterious.

Intentionally beginning a period of study in a prayerful way can help to balance a desire for knowledge and understanding with a willingness to be open-handed and non-grasping.

Practising

~ Choose a ritual that helps you become mindful of God with you. You may, for example, like to light a candle or go for a walk and bring back something that speaks to you of God or God's presence with you and in the world.

~ Reflect on what you hope to gain from this period of study. What are your central questions or concerns?

~ Ask God for whatever help you need to begin. For example, do you need the gift of concentration or clarity of thought? Do you desire openness or mental flexibility? Do you notice any anxiety or feelings of self-doubt that you need help with releasing?

~ You may also like to offer a spoken prayer to begin your time of study. Consider using Aquinas' prayer or my adapted version.

Aquinas' prayer for students: "Come, Holy Spirit, Divine Creator, true source of light and fountain of wisdom! Pour forth your brilliance upon my dense intellect, dissipate the darkness which covers me, that of sin and of ignorance. Grant me a penetrating mind to understand, a retentive memory, method and ease in learning, the lucidity to comprehend, and abundant grace in expressing myself. Guide the beginning of my work, direct its progress, and bring it to successful completion. This I ask through Jesus Christ, true God and true man, living and reigning with You and the Father, forever and ever. Amen."[14]

---

[14] For this and other prayers of Aquinas see *The Aquinas Prayer Book*, eds. Robert Anderson and Johann M. Moser (Nashua: Sophia Institute Press, 2000).

A creative adaptation of Aquinas' prayer: Come, Holy Spirit, source and giver of all light, and wisdom. May your joyful and creative love illuminate my mind and bring clarity to what is before me. Help me to notice, understand and remember what I study. Help me to stay focused and to enjoy the process. Help me to express myself clearly. I trust you to guide my work from beginning to end. Let it be what you intend it to be and grant me peace in accepting the journey, however it may unfold. I ask this through Jesus Christ who is always with me, strengthening, loving, and companioning me.

A note on studying texts or topics to study prayerfully

To study prayerfully is to seek God through learning and reflection. Any text or topic can be studied prayerfully but, if you are new to thinking of study as prayer, it may be easier for you to begin with something that you already recognise as carrying spiritual weight. Books on theology, philosophy, or spirituality are good places to start. Perhaps there is an issue that confuses or intrigues you that invites further study. Perhaps you are attracted by a spiritual practice and could learn more. Perhaps you feel drawn to learn more about a person of faith or a religious community. Try not to put limits on what you might study prayerfully in the future, instead focus on making a start with whatever seems to draw you at this time.

PRAYING TO END A PERIOD OF STUDY

Ending a period of study with prayer helps both to complete the process and to situate it in a wider experience of life and learning. It can help us to avoid the twin pitfalls of arrogance and anxiety by offering a space to express gratitude for the gift of our intellect and what has been learnt or understood, and to release any impulse to dominate or control. Ending with prayer helps us to accept, without shame, the provisional nature of our work and the limits of our intellects while simultaneously opening us to notice how we are being invited further along the journey of study. In turn, this helps us to hold our learning and thinking lightly while encouraging us to be open to the way we are being guided to deepen or share our knowledge and understanding.

Practising

~ Draw your attention back to whatever you offered yourself as a reminder of God's presence when you began your period of study. Become present to it again, receiving it as a witness to God's presence with you, whether or not you can sense it at this precise moment in time.

~ Reflect on what you have learnt. What seems significant? How do you feel about what you have learnt? Pay attention to bodily sensations as well as thoughts or emotions.

~ Ask God for help receiving your learning more deeply. Ask for the gift of trust that what is important for you will be retained and remembered. Ask, also, that what is not important for you be released, along with any anxiety or confusion that is unnecessary for your journey.

~ You may like to offer a spoken prayer. The following is a suggestion but you may like to write your own:

God of Light, Truth and Love,
I thank you for this time of prayer and study.
For your illumination, thank you.
For the wisdom of others, thank you.
For what I have learnt and understood, thank you.
For what will one day be revealed but for now
    remains hidden, thank you.
Help me to remain always a beginner, willing to learn
    and eager to receive.
Help me to let go of any desire to grasp or dominate.
May my learning bear fruit and become part of the
    unfolding revelation of your light, truth and love.
Amen.

INNER WRESTLING AS PRAYER

Having faith doesn't mean repressing questions and doubts but being willing to face them bravely and see them as situated in an ongoing and unfolding relationship with an ultimately mysterious God who always exceeds our grasp. As Ann Lamott writes, "The opposite of faith is not doubt, it's certainty."[15] Bravely facing the questions, the doubts and the discomfort sometimes means noticing them and patiently letting them be there; other times, it means a more active engagement through inner struggle or wrestling. This can involve thinking, remembering, reflecting, feeling, or any combination of these. Only you will know when it's time to move from one way of facing your doubts, questions and discomfort to the other, and both approaches have value.

---

[15] Ann Lamott, *Plan B: Further Thoughts on Faith* (Hull: Riverhead Books, 2006), 257.

This practice encourages you to notice and name your deepest questions or areas of struggle and offers a pathway to engaging with them with God. This with-ness is what makes this wrestling prayerful because it is offered in conversation with God who companions you in your questioning and doubting, as Jesus models with the disciples on the road to Emmaus.[16] Perhaps, though, it is this with-ness of God that you doubt. Perhaps you question the relationship with God itself. Even then, I believe that your wrestling can be prayerful. Sometimes it's only by releasing the relationship with God that we thought we had, that we can receive the relationship in its fullness, or in more of its fullness. This can take time and, at the releasing stage, it is common to have little or no hope that the relationship will return. Still, this releasing can be prayerful as it represents a refusal to settle for images of a too-small God. Resisting an urge to avoid the doubt and choosing to take an honest look at the real, is a choice of love over fear.

Practising

~ Begin by considering which issue or question causes you to wrestle. Without judgement, allow thoughts, words, or images to surface. Nothing is off limits. It could be academic or personal. It could be global in its reach or concern, or it could be something that affects only you or those closest to you. Perhaps there is a decision you need to make. Ask yourself: what is drawing my mental attention at this time?

~ Allow the issue(s) or question(s) to present themselves. Notice any discomfort and, if you can, welcome it as a sign that this is an area that needs to be brought in prayer.

~ Acknowledge God's presence with you, even if this feels mysterious or is believed or hoped for, rather than felt. See if you

---

[16] Luke 24:13-35.

can affirm, or open yourself to trusting, that God is able and willing to guide your thoughts and questions.

~ Allow yourself to think through the issue or question but, as you think, address your thoughts to God. Speak to God about the issue as you would talk to a friend. If it is helpful you can write your questions and thoughts.

~ Pause as you feel led.

~ Do not try to force understanding but keep addressing your thoughts and questions to God.

~ Welcome any insights but do not rush them.

~ Wait in the uncertainty, trusting, or seeking to trust, that you are not alone.

~ End with a spoken or silent prayer. If words feel out of reach, you may like to become present to your breathing and let it anchor you in this moment in time and at this particular place on your journey.

A Blessing for Those Who Are Wrestling
by Pierre Teilhard de Chardin[17]

Above all, trust in the slow work of God.
We are quite naturally impatient in everything to reach
    the end without delay.
We should like to skip the intermediate stages.
We are impatient of being on the way to something
    unknown, something new.
And yet it is the law of all progress
that it is made by passing through some stages of
    instability—
and that it may take a very long time.
And so I think it is with you;
your ideas mature gradually—let them grow,
let them shape themselves, without undue haste.
Don't try to force them on,
as though you could be today what time
(that is to say, grace and circumstances acting on your
    own good will)
will make of you tomorrow.
Only God could say what this new spirit
gradually forming within you will be.
Give Our Lord the benefit of believing
that his hand is leading you,
and accept the anxiety of feeling yourself
in suspense and incomplete.

---

[17] Pierre Teilhard de Chardin, "Patient Trust" from *Hearts on Fire*, ed. Michael Harter (Chicago: Loyola University Press, 2005), 102-103.

WONDER AS AN INVITATION
TO PRAYERFUL STUDY

Wonder is the beginning and end of research, reflection, and study. Without wonder, it's hard to know why we should bother; there has to be some curiosity or some intrigue to begin and motivate the process. Wonder also comes at the end when we experience when we find what we're searching for, when we reach that "aha" moment and are left marvelling. Although we can try to study without wonder (perhaps when we study to fulfil some bland requirement), we can only ever find and savour truth when we allow wonder to guide us. As David James Duncan writes: "We can seek truth without wonder's assistance - but seek is all we can do: there will be no finding. Until wonder descends, unlocks us, turns us slack-jawed... truth is unable to enter."[18]

This practice invites you to notice what you find wonder-ful and to allow it to guide you in an unhurried, heart-centred, and deeply prayerful journey of discovery. The journey is prayerful whatever the object of your study because God is both companion and destination: companion because this study is done with God's help and destination because as Truth, God is glimpsed through truth wherever it is found. To borrow St Augustine's words, prayerful study makes every topic a "stepping stone to things unperishable and everlasting."[19] Even if you can't see how your chosen topic of study might do that, try to suspend disbelief and trust wonder as a guide to what directs you towards God.

Practising
~ Reflect on what provokes wonder in you. What do you find wonder-ful? The mountains? Mushrooms? A child learning to speak? Medical progress? A feat of engineering? Even if you can't

---

[18] David James Duncan, *God Laughs and Plays: Churchless Sermons in Response to the Preachments of the Fundamentalist Right* (Great Barrington: Triad, 2007)
[19] Augustine, *Of True Religion* (Washington, DC: Regnery, 1991), xxix.

see the spiritual significance of what you are drawn to study or doubt whether it can be studied prayerfully, try to be open to being surprised.

~ Begin by setting an intention to study this topic with God. Acknowledge the Spirit as your companion. You might like to ask God to guide your study and to grant you openness to being led. You could also ask God to help you savour your study so you may be nourished by it. You may also like to offer a visible sign that this time is prayerful, for example by lighting a candle.

~ As you read or research, regularly pause and be attentive to what seems most important or meaningful.

~ Take time to linger in these noticings. Ask yourself how your learning speaks to you of God? What, or where, is God's invitation?

~ Close with gratitude, perhaps with a spoken or inward prayer. Take some time in silence, resting in God beyond thought and words.

long, honest look at the real. By "real" I mean who God is, who we are, and what is happening in our world.

If the idea of bodily positions guiding our attention seems strange, it is likely because we usually think that our minds lead and our bodies follow. And yet, when we consider concrete examples, it becomes clear that it is mostly the other way around. If we want to pay attention to a child, we have to get down to their level so that we can see into their eyes and let them know we are truly listening. If we want to read a book, we need to find somewhere to sit with good light. We can, of course, listen to our child or read a book without adopting these positions but we are more likely to miss something or to become distracted.

Interrupting our bodily patterns by intentionally moving them into a certain posture helps to bring us into the present moment and ready us for the work of attention. This work of becoming present is vital to prayer because it is in the present that we encounter God. Contrary to what we might sometimes believe, connecting with God isn't about detaching from the physical world or escaping time and space, it's about becoming aware of One who is already here, greeting us in *this* moment. Unlike our minds which can take us away into the remembered past or imagined future, our bodies are unavoidably rooted in the present. If we learn to listen, our bodies will always return us to the present moment where time seems to open up: we encounter eternity in time and enter God's presence.

> Connecting with God isn't about detaching from the physical world...it's about becoming aware of One who is already here.

My favoured positions for prayer have changed over time but those to which I've frequently returned are seated with upward facing palms, lying with forehead and forearms on the ground, outside with head tilted up to the sky. I find myself adopting these positions at times when words have seemed far away: when I've been tired, or when I've been overcome with gratitude or anxiety. And always these positions have allowed me to be before God beyond words or thoughts. I've experienced a sense of release and renewed my ability to be present to what is real, both within and around me. At these times, my body has guided my mind and soul into prayer.

Perhaps even more helpful as a gateway to prayer has been my breath. My breath has become both a reminder to pray and my prayer itself. If I've managed to follow Paul's advice to pray without ceasing at all, it is through prayerful breathing. The increasing popularity of breath-based meditation has made some Christians suspicious of the connection between breath and prayer (with the criticism being that it is an Eastern or new age practice). But it is a false dichotomy to pit Christianity against these: first, because it is unhelpful to place limits on when and how we may encounter God in the world and, second, because the connection between breath and God is very much central to Judeo-Christian theology. In Genesis 2:7 God breathes life into Adam establishing the connection between breath, life and relationship with God that is repeated throughout Scripture.[2]

This connection between breath and God is underlined by the mysterious name given to God in the Old Testament: YHWH (yod, he, vay and he). Scholars believe this name connects with the Hebrew verb "to be" - "hayah" – and also to the name Moses is given at the burning bush: "I am that I am" (also translated as "I will be what I will be").[3]

This name, though, is in itself unspeakable, being composed only of consonant sounds. Further, and as Richard Rohr notes, these are the only consonants in the Hebrew alphabet that are not articulated with lips and tongues. Rohr writes: "Many are convinced that [the

---

[2] For example, Isaiah 42:5, Job 33:4, Acts 17:25.
[3] Exodus 3:14.

tetragrammaton's] correct pronunciation is an attempt to replicate and imitate the very sound of inhalation and exhalation."[4]

YHWH, then, is a name that cannot be spoken but only breathed – with each of the sounds formed with a breath. To breathe is to have God's name on our lips: our very breathing invites us into prayer.

This connection between breath and prayer is underlined in the final verse of the Psalter: "Let everything that has breath praise the Lord."[5] While the rest of Psalm 150 encourages uninhibited and noisy prayer, the final verse has a different tone. Often this is missed, and it is seen as simply an affirmation of the preceding verses: that all creatures who breathe and are able should make noise to praise the Lord.

And yet, close attention to the final Hebrew word of the Psalm—"hallelujah"—suggests a different interpretation. This word, translated as "praise the Lord" is actually a two-word phrase: "Hallelu-yah" with "hallelu" meaning joyous praise and "yah" a shortened form of YHWH, a sound formed by an outward breath. The final Psalm of the Psalter, then, ends not with noisy praise offered by breathing beings but with breath itself, the outward breath of "yah", that is the very name of God. The implication seems to be that breath itself is already praise, and a worthy way of naming God. This interpretation is supported by the Hebrew word for "breath"—"nestima"—which is strikingly similar to the Hebrew for "soul"—"neshama."

> Breath is not trivial, it is soulful.

Breath is not trivial, it is soulful. The Psalm, then, invites us to praise God with song, dance and instruments, and also with our very breathing, which is at the core of our being, as essential to us as our souls. The phrase "Let everything that has breath praise the Lord" is a command not only to all living things to praise God but to praise God with every breath; it is an invitation for our breathing to *be* our rhythm of praise.

---

[4] Richard Rohr, *The Naked Now: Learning to See as the Mystics See* (New York: The Crossroad Publishing Company, 2009), 25.
[5] Psalm 150:6.

In following the invitation to praise God with breath, to allow my breath to guide my prayer, I have explored several practices including those offered within this chapter. These have been helpful in drawing my attention to my breath as an opening onto prayer but over time these words or practices have fallen away and now I find my breath itself speaks to God. As I become quiet and present to my breathing, I am reminded that my inhale is a breath of God's life and my exhale is the sound of God's name. In the space in between, I find that all thoughts of God as absent or distant are gone. Instead, I find that God is "closer... than breathing, and nearer than hands and feet."[6]

Our bodies' ability to guide and focus our attention and to bring us into the present moment where God is already present, is just one of the ways in which they have wisdom. Our bodies can also give us insight into what is happening within the deep places of ourselves— our unconscious desires and fears, our places of resistance and places of opening. Our bodies and minds are not opposed or even wholly distinct but, rather, intertwined. By attending to our bodies, we can begin to discover what is happening beneath the surface of ourselves.

The Irish theologian and poet John O'Donohue expresses this by saying that "there is a secret relationship between our physical being and the rhythm of our soul. The body is the place where the soul shows itself."[7] For O'Donohue, the body is not simply an external casing for the soul but a place where the soul reveals itself. The body is the "angel of the soul"[8] that both expresses and minds the soul. While we often struggle to understand ourselves or to mentally

---

[6] Lord Alfred Tennyson, "The Higher Pantheism" as quoted by The Poetry Foundation at https://www.poetryfoundation.org/poems/45323/the-higher-pantheism (accessed 4 April, 2022).
[7] John O'Donohue, *Anam Cara: Spiritual Wisdom from the Celtic World* (London: Bantam, 1999), 70.
[8] Ibid., 70.

untangle how things are with us, our bodies are waiting to teach us. As O'Donohue explains,

> "...the body rarely lies. Your mind can deceive you and put all kinds of barriers between you and your nature; but your body does not lie. Your body tells you, if you attend to it, how your life is and whether you are living from your soul or from the labyrinths of your negativity."[9]

In this passage, and others, O'Donohue encourages his reader to treat their body as a compass or wise friend and to attend to the body as a spiritual practice, noticing tension, energy, and ease as we let the body "speak". Like O'Donohue, I want to affirm that your body is a gift that offers a sacred opening onto others, the world and your hidden self. While listening to your body may be unfamiliar and feel strange at first, it's well worth persevering. The more we try to ignore our bodies, the more we will become disconnected from others, the natural world and, eventually, from ourselves.

Our bodies are gifts that offer a sacred opening onto others, the world and our hidden selves.

Ignoring our bodies will also mean becoming disconnected from God. As embodied beings we have been created to encounter God's presence not only with our minds and hearts but in and though our bodies. While many Christian writers have denigrated the body, the writings and examples of flesh-affirming mystics such as Julian of Norwich, can be very helpful in learning to receive our bodies as profound places of encounter that draw us further along the path of our journey into ever deepening relationship with God. These champions of the sanctity of the body take as their inspiration and guide Jesus, whose body was a place of encounter with God both for himself and for others. Jesus didn't practise bodily denial or

---

[9] Ibid., 73.

rejection but embraced his physicality. He didn't remain statically in one place but moved from town to town, climbing mountains, walking across land and water, moving ever closer to Jerusalem and to his very real, physical death. He enjoyed eating and drinking with others and knew when he needed to rest. These bodily actions weren't superfluous to his ministry but were moments of revelation of God in flesh and each embodied action affirms to his followers the original goodness of the body. And, let's remember: it was through touch and tears and spit and blood that Jesus healed and drew others towards himself and to God.

It may, though, be difficult to pray with our bodies. When we're sick or in pain or we compare our bodies to others and find ours lacking we may feel our bodies have betrayed us. Or perhaps we feel we have betrayed our bodies by neglecting, rejecting or abusing them. But however hurt, wounded or inadequate we may believe our bodies to be, they remain our closest companions and our most intimate friends, whose very physicality has already been named "good" by God.[10] No matter their story or our feelings towards them, our bodies are worthy of our attention and care. What's more, our bodies don't need to be healthy for them to be an opening onto God. Indeed, it's in Jesus' broken body revealed on the cross and shared in the eucharist that we see and taste the love of God.

These practices invite you to see your body as a place of spiritual encounter. In the following pages, you will find encouragement to play with praying in different positions, with your breath, and with your senses. You will be offered the opportunity to see your bodily sensations, whatever they may be, as openings onto prayer rather than distractions or disturbances. The goal of these isn't to replace the role of the mind in prayer with that of the body, but to encourage you to embrace your embodiment as you come before God and seek a closer relationship with the One who declares that you are "fearfully and wonderfully made."[11]

---

[10] Genesis 1:31.
[11] Psalm 139:14.

For reflection

Which positions do you most associate with prayer?

How does your body help you to pay attention?

When have you experienced God in or through your body?

In what ways might your body invite prayer?

PRAYING IN DIFFERENT POSITIONS

Perhaps you already have a posture you favour for prayer but if you don't or you sense a nudge to play with posture, you may find it helpful to experiment with different positions, noticing how they affect your prayer as well as your willingness and ability to attend. Over time, you may come to associate a certain posture so closely with attending to God that simply adopting this posture becomes your prayer and words slip away.

Practising

~ Become present to this moment by using your breath. Acknowledge God's presence with you and your intention to be with God here and now.

~ How are you being invited to move your body? Let yourself be guided into a position. If you feel resistance, scan the list of suggested positions below and see if anything draws your attention or curiosity.

~ You can either pray as you would usually pray or let your prayer be your willingness to move your body into this position. In both cases, focus on your breathing which will anchor you into awareness of this moment where God is always waiting to greet you.

~ End as you began: with your breath and an acknowledgement that God is with you.

Some Positions for Prayer

~ Standing up
~ Lying on the floor on your back
~ With palms facing up
~ With arms lifted high
~ Kneeling
~ With your forehead touching the floor
~ Lying face down with arms outstretched

BODY PRAYER OF JULIAN OF NORWICH

This simple practice joins four postures with words: await, allow, accept, and attend. Some sources claim that Julian of Norwich originated the prayer, but most agree that it is a contemporary body prayer that uses four key words from the motto of the Order of Julian of Norwich. Either way, this practice is thoroughly in keeping with Julian of Norwich's spirituality since her body was so central to her experience and understanding of God.[12]

This practice invites you to embrace your physicality as a pathway into stillness. It offers an embodied way of grounding yourself in the presence of God and of becoming more aware of how divine love may be nudging you.

Practising
~ Begin by standing up and straightening your back and neck.

---

[12] In May 1373, Julian became extremely ill and had a series of experiences of God's love that she experienced not in spite of but through her bodily suffering. In her book about the experiences, *The Revelations of Divine Love*, she uses bodily imagery to describe God, God's love and the life of prayer.

~ Cup your hands together in front of you at waist height as a sign of your openness to receive. Say aloud or inwardly: await.

~ Await God's presence. Let go of any expectation, hope or imagining of what might happen.

~ Reach your hands up and outwards as a sign of your willingness to be with what is. Say aloud or inwardly: allow.

~ Allow a sense of God's presence (or not) to come to you. Let it be what it is, without forcing it to meet your hopes or expectations.

~ Cup your hands towards your body and move them towards your heart. Say aloud or inwardly: accept.

~ Accept that you are not in control. Accept that God is present, whether you are aware of it or not.

~ Stretch your hands out in front of you. Say aloud or inwardly: attend.

~ Attend to what you are called to be or to do. Attend to how God is inviting you to move from this stance of openness.

FOCUSING PRAYER

Two recent champions of the body and its wisdom are the Jesuit priests Fathers Edwin McMahon and Peter Campbell. Deeply convinced of the sacred significance of the body and importance of physicality in the spiritual life, the pairing founded the biospiritual institute to teach the practice of biospiritual focusing. The methodology of this practice was first developed by philosophy professor Eugene Gendlin but was adapted and popularised by McMahon and Campbell in the 1980s. It is in keeping with Jesus' own approach to the body as worthy of honour and attention[13] and offers a way to listen to places within our bodies that are hurt physically, emotionally, or spiritually by creating a space for them to "speak" to us and tell us what they know and what they need. As McMahon and Campbell explain, since our bodies hold the energy of our life experiences and connect us with the universe and God who sustains all, paying attention to them allows us to access their inner wisdom and can be a way of listening for and responding to God's movement in our lives. They write: "BioSpiritual Focusing is a spiritual practice that centers on developing the habit of noticing and nurturing the inner wisdom of our bodies that connects us to the wider Cosmos and the Divine. It opens up the 'body' side of our spirituality."[14]

Practising

~ Find a comfortable place to be still for 20-40 minutes. Begin by acknowledging God's presence with you and ask for help noticing what is asking to be noticed.

~ Close your eyes and breathe deeply. Let your attention settle deep within your body.

~ Either scan your body from head to toe, noticing each part and what is present within it, or ask yourself which part of your body wants your attention right now. Keep scanning or asking until you identify an area that seems to be particularly charged, either

---

[13] In the Gospels, Jesus recognises and responds to bodily needs, noticing when he and others need to eat, retreat and rest. He honours the physicality of those he meets by feeding them, healing them, and even washing their feet. It's through touch that he heals and this touch isn't merely symbolic gesture but a real source of power.

[14] From McMahon and Campbell's website www.biospiritual.org. You can find out more about BioSpirituality and BioSpiritual Focusing here and in their book *BioSpirituality: Focusing as a Way to Grow* (Chicago: Loyola, 1985).

with pain or some other felt sense of significance, perhaps through tingling or warmth or simply because it draws your attention. Don't rush this step; give yourself as much time as you need.

~ Ask this bodily part or feeling if it is alright to go further. Respect it if it says no; you can always return to the practice later. Be gentle with your body.

~ Bring your full awareness to this bodily part or feeling. How would you describe it? Is there an image or word or colour or emotion?

~ Continue to sit with your bodily part or feeling without judgement. Simply observe it. Notice if anything else emerges.

~ Ask the body part or feeling what it needs. Ask it to show you how healing would feel.

~ You may want to offer this part of you some warmth by placing your hand on it. You may also want to ask God to help you care for this part of you.

~ Gently end the conversation by thanking the part of your body that has "spoken" and God for the gift of this body part and its wisdom.

THREE WAYS TO PRAY WITH BREATH

In the Judeo-Christian tradition, breath and Spirit are closely aligned. The Hebrew word "ruach" means breath, spirit or wind and we first encounter it in Genesis 1:2 when the "ruach" of God sweeps over the face of the waters. It is related to the very breath that makes Adam a living creature, joining human life with God's own life. Spirit, life and breath, then, are all intimately entwined and all open onto each other. For this reason, breath can be viewed as a constant invitation to pray, to become present to Life and Spirit flowing through us. There are many ways to follow this invitation and these practices are offered only as suggestions. As you become more familiar with attending to your breath, you will likely discover more ways to follow your breath's invitation.

Practising

A. *Offering Breath as Presence and Praise*
As mentioned in the introduction to this chapter, the mysterious and unspeakable name for God (the tetragrammaton) is composed of four Hebrew letters that are formed with breath. The implication seems to be that our breath is, in some sense, God's name and that our breathing already has a prayerful shape. This breath prayer builds on this foundation and invites you to bring your attention to your breath as divine naming and to offer your breathing as prayer. It is a way to follow Psalm 150's exhortation: "Let everything that has breath praise the Lord."[15]

~ Acknowledge your intent to praise God with your breath. You may like to remember that the breath of God is the life within you and acknowledge your breath as the sign of that life.

~ As you breathe, bring your full attention to your inhale and your exhale. To accentuate this, breathe in through your nose and out through your mouth. You may like to hold up a hand in front of your face so you can feel your breath as you exhale.

---

[15] Psalm 150:6.

~ Notice the sensation as you draw in air, the fullness between inhale and exhale, the sensation of release as you exhale and the emptiness between exhale and inhale.

~ Resist the urge to analyse or reflect. This can happen later but, for now, stay present to your breathing.

~ If you like, you can try sounding "Yah" on one outward breath and "Weh" on the next. This may help you to acknowledge the prayerful shape of your breathing.

~ Close with gratitude, perhaps with a final, deeper breath that fills you with the gift of life and a long exhale that speaks God's name.

B. Offering Breath as Meditation

Breath also invites prayer by guiding and deepening reflection. By keeping our attention focused on the pattern of breath, we interrupt any tendency to over-analyse and allow whatever it is that we are reflecting on to descend from head to heart and be received and integrated in a deep way, perhaps more deeply than our conscious awareness. This practice can be combined with *lectio divina* or the Jesus prayer; you will simply need to alter the words that are offered with inhale and exhale.

~ Begin by deciding what you would like to meditate on. Ideally, it will be short enough to be inwardly spoken with one round of inhalation and exhalation. A scriptural verse is a good place to start (for example, "The Lord is my shepherd/ I shall not want") but any phrase that centres your attention on God or with which you feel a deep resonance can be used.

~ Take one deep, cleansing breath and offer this as your intention to meditate with your breath.

~ With your next inhale, inwardly speak the first half of your phrase.

~ In the fullness between inhale and exhale, let those words sink deeper.

~ With your exhale, inwardly speak the second half of your phrase.

~ In the emptiness between exhale and the next inhale, let those words sink deeper.

~ Continue this pattern of breathing and inwardly speaking as long as you would like.

~ End with a final breath or Amen but remember that you can return to this pattern of breathing and meditating throughout your day.

C. Offering Breath as Intercession

If you sometimes find yourself overwhelmed by the number of people or situations you want to remember in prayer, you may find this practice helpful. I increasingly find myself offering intercession using this practice because it is neither forced nor prescriptive and yet expands the parameters of my prayer.

~ Close your eyes and take a deep breath. Open yourself to receive the faces and situations for which you are being invited to pray.

~ As you inhale let the first face or image present itself. Don't force it, let it offer itself. If nothing comes, that's ok. Keep breathing.

~ Resist the temptation to analyse why that face or image has offered itself. Instead, let it take shape as you continue with your inhale.

~ Hold that face or image in the fullness between inhale and exhale.

~ As you exhale, gently release the face or image. You may find it helpful to do this releasing through inwardly offering a spoken prayer or blessing. For example, "Lord, have mercy" or "God bless."

~ Let the space between exhale and inhale be empty.

~ With your next inhale, allow another face or image to present itself. If the same face or image offers itself, let it happen. Don't try to change it. Keep receiving, holding and releasing it until something else presents itself.

~ Close with a final deep breath. You may like to visualise all of the people and situations being gathered, held and released.

PRAYING WITH OUR SENSES

"Taste and see that the Lord is good." Psalm 34:8

Usually, these words are read metaphorically but they can also be understood literally if we take seriously passages such as Psalm 104 and Romans 1:20, which seem to imply that God is revealed in the sensuousness of creation. This practice is inspired by Psalm 34:8

and invites you to experience God not only with your mind and heart but with your body and, in particular, your senses.

Practising

~ Find a comfortable position or consider going for a walk. Review your day or become present to your surroundings. As you consult each of your senses, ask yourself: where is God? If you are reviewing your day, you might ask yourself: "When have I seen God?" Or, if you are becoming present to your surroundings, you might ask yourself: "Where can I see God?"

~ Move through all of your senses in this way: sight, hearing, smell, touch and taste. If nothing offers itself, don't force it but be open to being surprised; try not to shut down the possibility that God has been in your sensing by refusing to ask the question.

~ If you feel resistance to the idea of sensing God, trying replacing "God" with "the goodness of God" or "God's presence" or "love".

~ Offer whatever comes in prayer. You may like to give thanks for the times you have in some way experienced God with your body. You may also like to ask for increased awareness of the sensory moments that reveal something of God to you.

PRAYING WITH A CUP OF COFFEE OR TEA

This practice invites you to turn your daily cup of coffee or tea into a prayerful experience by allowing your senses to companion you into the moment where God is already present and in which you can speak and listen freely.

Practising

~ As you begin, ask to have your senses readied to find God in this encounter.

~ Look: What do you notice about your cup? What colour is your tea or coffee? Is the liquid moving or still? Can you see steam? What else can you see? Take a moment to rest in your sense of sight.

~ Listen: What do you hear in this space? Can you hear anything outside? What do you hear in yourself? Take a moment to rest in your sense of hearing.

~ Touch: What does it feel like to hold your cup? Is it rough or smooth? Is it warm or cold? Allow the sensation to travel through your hands and arms into your whole body. Take a moment to rest in your sense of touch.

~ Smell: Take a deep inhale. What do you smell? Exhale slowly and then take another deep inhale closer to your cup. What do you smell? Exhale slowly and take a moment to rest in your sense of smell.

~ Taste: Take a small sip of your drink. Allow it to rest in your mouth for a moment before you swallow. What can you taste? Take a bigger sip and, again, allow it to sit in your mouth. Try moving it around with your tongue. What else can you taste? Swallow and take a moment to rest in your sense of taste.

~ As you move your attention to your centre, rest in the knowledge that God is here in this moment.

~ At this point you may become aware of something that is asking to be shared with or spoken to God. If so, speak freely, either inwardly or aloud. You may also find yourself becoming aware of something God is offering to you—some inner nudge or knowing. If nothing comes, simply let yourself rest in the moment and allow your consent to be present to be your prayer.

~ Close with thanksgiving: for this moment, for your body and its senses, for water, coffee and tea, for all those whose work has made possible this moment.

Sensory Prayer in the Everyday

You can pray in this way with all sorts of everyday activities. Simply let your senses guide you into the present by consulting each of them in turn, then become aware of what is asking to be shared with God, and end with gratitude.

Suggestions for everyday activities that invite this kind of prayer include:
  ~ Going for a walk
  ~ Brushing your teeth
  ~ Washing your hands
  ~ Making dinner: chopping, stirring, etc.
  ~ Folding laundry
  ~ Gardening

Praying with the Story of Our Lives

I have a friend who is fond of saying, "We all have a book in us." She means that everyone has the capacity to write one book during their life; perhaps you will agree, perhaps not. Either way, the deeper truth to my friend's perspective is that we all carry stories within us: the stories of our lives. The story within is a story that is lived rather than written and those who do translate their lived stories into print can never do so completely because the stories of our lives on earth are only finished when we die. Even then, it's only our earthly story that is finished. As C. S. Lewis puts it at the end of his Narnia series, death isn't the end but only the "beginning of Chapter One of the Great Story which no one on earth has read: which goes on forever: in which every chapter is better than the one before."[1]

If the plot of the story of your life is the unfolding sequence of events in your life, the characters are all those whose lives are intertwined with yours. Perhaps you see yourself as the main character in your life's story or perhaps you give this role to another. But you are always the narrator of the story and all of who you are helps to tell it: your body and the marks it carries, your memories, your dreams, your hopes, your thoughts, your patterns of behaviour, your sense of humour and so much more.

Because we are inseparably bound up with our story, there's a sense in which we can't help but tell it. And yet the urge to give words to our story is powerful. In my experience, this urge becomes particularly strong with transformative experiences that push the limits of our understanding, challenge our assumptions or seem to demand a response.

When I was pregnant with Henry, I joined a couple of antenatal groups. The women from these groups became close friends and an

---

[1] C. S Lewis, *The Last Battle* (London: HarperCollins, 2015), 172.

invaluable source of comfort and encouragement in the weeks, months and years following. As we got to know each other, we shared snippets of our stories but it was only after our children were born that we really leaned into story-telling as a mode of friendship. One by one, we would share our labour stories as a way of processing what had happened to us, body, mind and spirit. We didn't spare the details and, considering we had only recently met, it was surprising how willing we were to be vulnerable. And yet in the telling there was healing. Our collective experience of labour and birth meant we were easily able to hold space for each other to share. We had patience with, and compassion for, one another and understood the need to tell our story and often at great length. In telling my story to these women, I was able to give shape and structure to the events, to process the facts and emotions and eventually to accept what had happened as a new part of my story and my emerging identity as mother.

Since then, I've experienced a similar unburdening through storytelling with these women and with other friendship groups. These friends have held open a space in which to share joy and gratitude, disappointment and frustration, sadness and anger. Insights have been gained, tension and fear released, and all has been eased along with tears and hugs and laughter. All human beings need friends like this and I hope you have yours. As Aristotle writes, "No one would choose to live without friends even if he had all the other goods."[2]

Yet, while a good friend's value is inestimable, I've found that the one I really long to tell my story to is God. Not as a distant figure removed from the events of my life but one who is deeply and lovingly present with me in and through it all. I long to tell my story to God because God is the one who knows and loves me most intimately, the one who illuminates my path and guides me in the journey of my life. No human being can offer me the same space in which to be myself, nor the same degree of attention, nor the same depth of healing. To expect this is to expect too much. If I feel a

---

[2] Aristotle, *Nicomachean Ethics* (Oxford: OUP, 2009), 1155a.

friend has offered me something approaching this space, I know that God is somehow at work in and through them and their companionship.

To pray with our lives, then, means to tell our story to God. It means to be honest with God about where we've been, where we are and where we long to be. This is important, not because we're telling God something God wouldn't otherwise know but because telling our story to God helps us to claim our story at the same time as we surrender it, accept it while acknowledging we are not in control of it. We name the peaks and troughs, our joy and pain, and yet also learn not to force understanding or healing but to release our grip on a need for meaning and lean into trusting that, somehow, all shall be revealed and made well in time. This work of naming and situating is often what praying with our lives looks like. Like a child carefully choosing and then dropping pebbles into a lake, we reflect on our lives and notice what is asking to be named and intentionally brought into God's presence. Sometimes it's an event that asks to be brought, sometimes a feeling or thought. And like a child watching the ripples of that sinking pebble, we can also linger to notice what happens when that event or feeling is named and offered. Sometimes a deep peace will ripple through us, sometimes an invitation or conviction may offer itself in return. Sometimes what has been named will stubbornly refuse to be released, and asks to be held longer or gently released again.

To pray with our lives...means to tell our story to God.

To pray with our lives not only means bringing our lives to God but also receiving our lives as the place where we meet God; the place where God greets us, invites us, and guides us. It means resisting the thought that God is up there and we are down here, instead embracing God here, already with us. That doesn't just mean in the neat, tidy places of our lives or in the moments that feel particularly spiritual but in the whole of our life as it unfolds, including the losses, the challenges and the failures. God is in all of life, and all and any of it is a place of encounter. To quote Paula D'Arcy, "God comes to you disguised as your life."[3]

Learning to recognise God in the disguise of our lives is a work of discernment, of seeking to recognise God's presence in the givenness of our lives and how we might respond to that presence. This may be easier to do at some times than at others but it doesn't mean God is only disguised in those times of easier discernment. Paula D'Arcy was twenty-seven years old and three months pregnant when a drunk driver killed both her husband and her one-year-old child and yet she doesn't tell us "God comes to you disguised *in certain parts of* your life" but "God comes to you disguised as your life."

This work of discernment is set before each of us and we need nothing more than the material of our lives to get started. You may find that free writing in a journal is the most useful practice. For others, the structure of the Ignatian practice of the examen is helpful. Both practices are included in this chapter.

I've found, though, that what has really encouraged and enabled me to tell my story to God has been meeting with a spiritual director. Spiritual direction has ancient roots, and in the Christian tradition stretches back through the monastic tradition to the desert fathers and mothers of the third century. It has evolved through the centuries and although there are many varieties of spiritual director, all seek to offer a safe space in which a directee can explore their spiritual journey, with all its light and shadow. It is a way of caring for souls that is tender, personal and confidential.

Spiritual direction is sometimes confused with counselling because it involves meeting with someone to talk about life and the questions it presents. The focus, however, is different from counselling. The aim is not to fix or solve or even, surprisingly, to direct but, rather, to companion a person deeper into their life's experiences and to help them attend to God's guiding, directive presence with them: to receive their lives as God's disguise.

---

[3] Cited in Richard Rohr, *Falling Upwards: A Spirituality for the Two Halves of Life* (London: SPCK, 2012), 66.

While the one listening holds the title "spiritual director" the real director is the Spirit. The spiritual director's role is to hold open the space so that the Spirit's movements can be noticed and to encourage the directee to be guided by them. Spiritual directors, then, don't have an agenda, they help to make it safe for a person to go where the Spirit is nudging them, even if that is into deeper, darker places. As Barbara Brown Taylor explains of the difference between pastoral counsellors and spiritual directors, "We go to counsellors when we want help getting out of caves. We go to directors when we are ready to be led farther in."[4]

God is in all of life, and all and any of it is a place of encounter.

Spiritual direction has helped me to learn to be more honest with God, to explore my experience of God and life without censure. It has helped me to learn to stay with my feelings, to trust my experience as a place of encounter and to listen for the inner wisdom of the indwelling Spirit. I think, though, that the main fruit of my experience of receiving spiritual direction, has been a greater readiness to tell my story to God; to receive the givens of my life as the place where God meets me and invites me to respond. While you don't need a spiritual director to tell your story to God, it can be an immense help and if you find yourself struggling to tell your story to God, or these practices stir in you a greater longing to tell or explore your story, you might like to consider seeking out a director.

Even if we know there are experiences that need to be told to God and we long to receive our lives as a place of encounter, we may feel resistance to the idea of praying with the story of our lives. Perhaps it's because it seems self-indulgent and we think that we should be more outward looking. Maybe wrapped up in this is the belief that reviewing life is a negative thing. Many of us have been warned

---

[4] Barbara Brown Taylor, *Learning to Walk in the Dark: Because God Often Shows Up at Night* (London: HarperOne, 2015), 129.

about the danger of looking back with rose tinted glasses or becoming consumed with regret. Perhaps we worry we'll get stuck in the past and fail to be present to our lives as they are now.

In my experience, however, it's the practice of remembrance that prevents life from feeling like a series of disconnected events. Often, it's only when I look back that I can see a pattern and purpose and begin to discern the way in which my story is entwined in God's story. I notice the times I've said yes to God and when I've turned away, I see the ways in which God has been inviting me into relationship again and again, whether I've said yes or not. I discover past prayers have been answered, although perhaps in unexpected ways. I gather together the pieces of my life and find the golden thread of God's presence with me through it all.

My experience of the importance of remembrance echoes the practice as it's found in the Bible. Amongst other figures, both David and Paul model the practice of remembrance as a way of becoming more aware of how God is forming them in and through their stories. In many of the Psalms, David remembers his story, with all its joy and sorrow and gains a deeper awareness of the ways in which God meets him in both states. This awareness doesn't flatten the highs and lows of life but encourages a greater openness to receive these states as places of encounter with God. In Acts, Paul recounts how his life was dramatically interrupted by Jesus on the road to Damascus and offers this story to the crowd as the foundation of both his new identity and mission.[5] In his letters to the early Christian communities, he reflects on how this interruption shifted his understanding of what is precious and worthy of pursuit, encouraging others to review their own values.[6]

Perhaps, though, you struggle more with the idea of thinking about or praying for the future. It's easy to worry that if we name our hearts' desires we leave ourselves vulnerable to disappointment. While it *is* risky and bold to pray with our hearts' deepest desires, it is also necessary if we're to be honest in our relationship with God.

---

[5] See Acts 22.
[6] See Philippians 3.

Again, the Bible encourages us. In the Old Testament, the people of God cry out for the Messiah to save them and, in the New Testament, they long for Jesus' return and the completion it will bring.

While I hope this helps to temper any concerns about praying with past and future, I agree that it's wise to be wary of spending all our time in the past and future. There's value in looking both backwards and forwards but it's only healthy to do so when we have a firm rooting in the present moment. The present is our home in time and the place from which we pivot to look to the past and to the future. At the communion table, we remember and we look forward, but the command "do this" tells us to be a people of action in the present moment.[7] Ultimately, telling the story of our lives means looking for how God is here now and becoming aware of how and where we are being invited in this particular moment.

The practices in this chapter take different approaches to praying with the story of our lives. All you need to begin is some material from your unfolding story and a willingness to look, or try to look, honestly at it. They all encourage you to notice, name, release and receive, but offer different pathways to do this. Wherever and however you feel led to begin to tell your story to God, may you know that you are loved and seen and that God is making all things new, your story included.

---

[7] Luke 22:19.

Do you think of your life as a story? What title would you give the story of your life?

With whom do you feel safe to tell the story of your life?

When telling your story, is it harder to look to the past, present or future?

THE EXAMEN

This spiritual exercise, also called the examination of consciousness, helps us to grow continually in noticing—or discerning—God's presence in our everyday life. Developed in the sixteenth century by Ignatius of Loyola, founder of the Jesuit order, the examen encourages a prayerful review of the day. Ignatius of Loyola considered the examen to be the single most important spiritual practice and one of his few rules of prayer for the Jesuit order was the requirement that Jesuits practise the examen twice daily: at noon and at the end of the day.

The examen has evolved over time and there are now many iterations available to Jesuits and non-Jesuits alike. It's especially well-suited to the end of the day or the beginning of the day (looking back at the day before) but can be prayed at any time. Through prayerful consideration of the day's experiences, the examen creates a space to discern how God has been present in both the high and low points of the day. In such a space, all experiences are viewed in the light of God's love, including: tasks, relationships, daydreams, attitudes, surprises, thought processes, moments of clarity, moments of confusion, joys and disappointments. The examen asks God to illuminate both those areas that draw our gratitude and celebration and those areas that need forgiveness and healing. The latter isn't meant to encourage shame, self-rejection or self-punishment but to highlight where we are being asked to let go so that we may experience love's healing.

If you begin to practise the examen regularly, you'll likely find that it helps you to gain a deeper appreciation of the intimate presence of God in your life, even its messy or shadowy aspects. You will also exercise your discernment muscles as you notice where you are following love's invitation and where you are experiencing resistance.[8]

Practising

~ Begin by asking for the grace to see yourself and your day in the light of God's love. Ask for help receiving whatever you find in your day that has been a gift or seems to be in the flow of love and releasing whatever you find that seems to be out of step with or working against love.

~ Replay your day and notice what you're grateful for. Let your mind wander over your day and try to pinpoint specific moments that make you thankful. It may be helpful to name them, either by writing them down or by stating them inwardly. For example, "the hot cup of coffee that smelt so good", "the conversation that went better than I had hoped," or "the passerby who smiled at me." The more specific you can be in naming these, the more you

---

[8] For more on the examen see *Rummaging for God* by Dennis Hamm, *What is Ignatian Spirituality?* by David L. Fleming, and *Sleeping with Bread* by Matthew Linn, Sheila Fabricant Linn and Francisco Miranda.

will be able to receive and hold onto them. Give yourself some time to savour again these moments.

~ Replay your day again, this time paying attention to your feelings throughout the day. As Jesuit priest Dennis Hamm says, "Feelings...are clear signals of where the action was in the day."[9] So, try to notice which emotions you felt particularly intensely. Try not to filter out anything uncomfortable; instead, let yourself become present to whatever was there within you today (including delight, fear, anticipation, boredom, resentment, anger, peace, contentment, anxiety, impatience, desire, hope, regret, shame, uncertainty, compassion, disgust, gratitude, pride, rage, doubt, confidence, admiration, and shyness). If you struggle to connect with your feelings, you could also notice when your thoughts seemed particularly loud or when your body responded strongly.

~ Which feeling particularly caught your attention or seemed significant? If this is difficult, ask God to bring it to the surface and go with whatever comes, even if you're not sure it's the "right" one.

~ What do you want to say to God about this feeling? Is this feeling attached to a moment in your day when you felt in step or out of step with God, when you felt you were being led by God's love or when you were resisting God's love? Talk to God freely about this feeling. Don't say what you think you should say but let your prayer be spontaneous. You might want to offer praise or ask for help or forgiveness or healing.

---

[9] Dennis Hamm, 'Rummaging for God: Praying Backwards Through Your Day' in *America*, 14 May, 1994; accessed on 4 April, 2022 at https://www.ignatianspirituality.com/ignatian-prayer/the-examen/rummaging-for-god-praying-backward-through-your-day/

~ Look forward to tomorrow. Bring to mind what activities, events, tasks or appointments lie before you. Use your calendar, if you need help with remembering.

~ What feelings surface as you look at what is facing you tomorrow? Do you feel afraid, excited, delighted, doubtful, bored, regretful, weak, brave? Again, talk to God freely about this feeling. Let the prayer be spontaneous.

~ End with some deep, refreshing breaths as you rest in God's promise to be with you.

WALKING THE LABYRINTH

Walking a labyrinth offers an embodied way to pray the story of our lives. A labyrinth is an ancient Christian prayer practice that involves walking a winding path that leads to a central place and that then winds back out to the point where it began. It isn't a maze so there are no dead ends and no sense of it being a challenge. The path is symbolic of the journey towards God's indwelling presence and illumination and then outward, grounded in the knowledge of God's presence and empowered to act in the world. It can help us to reflect on our spiritual journey as we enact it.

Traditionally, the three stages of the labyrinth are purgation, illumination and union which correspond to the inward, centre and outward portions of the walk. There are, however, various ways to interpret these stages and the labyrinth can be walked in many ways, some of which are offered in Lauren Atress' book *Walking a Sacred Path: Rediscovering the Labyrinth as a Spiritual Practice*.

The labyrinth practice included here is simple and intends to help you become aware of what is asking to be released, received, and resolved at this present point in your life's story. It can be walked using a permanent labyrinth or a temporary labyrinth. If you can't find or create a labyrinth, you can walk a version of the labyrinth using a loop of your neighbourhood, moving closer to a central point and then further away. In her book *50 Ways to Pray* Teresa Blythe also suggests meandering in and out of the pews of a church with the front of the church as the centre. For those unable to walk, finger labyrinths can offer a way to access this practice. You simply trace the path of a printed labyrinth with your finger, reflecting on the journey as you go.

Practising

~ Before you begin, take some time to check-in with yourself. What bodily sensations are there? What emotions do you notice? What hopes or expectations or doubts are you carrying? Don't try to change them, just be aware of what is true of you, right now.

~ Express inwardly your intention to be present to this practice and to be open to being led deeper into your life and God's presence. Ask God for help with this.

~ As you move towards the centre, meditate on releasing. What is asking to be released so you can rest with God in this place in the story of your life? What no longer serves you? What do you need to let go?

~ As you sit or stand quietly in the centre, meditate on receiving. What is God offering to you? What is for you to receive? If nothing comes, let yourself simply rest in quiet and stillness, trusting that God offers you love and peace, whether or not you are aware of it or are able to receive it.

~ As you slowly walk outwards from the centre, meditate on resolving. What is for you to do as you continue on with the story of your life? How are you being asked to engage the world, grounded in the blessings you have received? What does it mean for you to resolve to do that?

~ Before you step away from the labyrinth, take a moment to honour your journey, perhaps with a bow.

FINDING YOUR LIFE'S COMPASS

When facing major decisions or in periods of boredom, disillusionment or confusion, it can be helpful to take a wider look at life. This practice is based on an exercise in *The Enduring Heart: Spirituality for the Long Haul* by Wilke Au and is intended to help you reflect on the bigger picture of your life, looking backwards and forwards from where you are now. It asks that you sit with various questions as you consider different aspects of yourself and your life. It may help you to gain clarity on the overall shape and direction of your story which, in turn, may help to bring greater understanding about specific challenges or areas of struggle. It's a good idea to repeat this practice regularly, perhaps annually, as a way of staying present to your unfolding story. This can help you to identify growth or change as well as any patterns of grasping or resistance that call for healing.

Practising

~ Using a large piece of blank paper, draw a large circle and divide it into four quadrants representing the four directions: south and north, east and west. In the centre, draw a smaller circle and leave this space open as your place to stand and look in each direction.

~ Label the segments using the headings below and add words and images in response to the questions. Try to do this without judgement, trusting that what comes is worthy of being named. You may also find yourself drawn to create a collage using found objects, pictures and photographs. The order in which you complete the quadrants is up to you, the following is just a suggestion. You will likely find it easier to look in some directions than in others. Don't try to force any reflections, instead pay attention to any enthusiasm or resistance and ask where these feelings may come from.

~ *West: the direction of the setting sun and of endings and letting go.*
   What practices or patterns drain you of energy?
   What are you holding onto that no longer works for you?
   What needs to be released, ended or shed?

~ *East: the direction of the rising sun and of new beginnings.*
   Is there something new that is attempting to catch your attention?
   Is there new energy and/or movement starting to emerge in you that you now need or want to embrace?
   Are there issues or behaviours in need of attention or change?

~ *South: the direction of sunny exposure, of energy, imagination, spontaneity and play.*
   When, where and with whom do you find it easiest to be yourself?
   Where is your creative energy wanting to find expression?
   Where do you find fun, play and rest?
   What warms your soul, spirit, life?

How do you nurture yourself?

~ *North: the direction of guidance, of guiding light and stabilising forces.*

Where can you turn when you need stability in your life?

Who deeply loves you and guides you?

Who are your spiritual guides and deepest friends?

What are the images or pictures of God or from Scripture that nurture and sustain you?

What is the grace story from your life and/or Scripture that enlivens you?

~ *Centre: a place of deeper reflection over all of the compass directions.*

Review your completed compass by offering your attention to what has emerged and by taking some time to reflect on the process creating it. You may like to reflect on the following questions:

What draws your eye or causes you to pause?

Does anything about your completed compass surprise you?

What patterns or echoes do you notice?

Which quadrant was easiest to complete? Which was hardest? How do you know this?

What was it like to move between looking in different directions? Did any shift feel particularly natural or awkward?

~ If you feel your compass truthfully reflects where you are right now, see if you are able to write "yes" in the centre circle as an affirmation to commit yourself, with God's help, to living by your compass. This is your intention to release what is ending, step into what is beginning, embrace joy, and be guided by God.

~ If you feel resistance to writing "yes" at the centre (perhaps because something on your compass troubles you), what do you want to write in the centre?

FREE WRITING AS A SPIRITUAL PRACTICE

In *Journaling as a Spiritual Practice*, Helen Cepero explains that journaling can help us to go beneath the surface of our lives in order to discover that "God is already present in the hidden depths of the present moment."[10] When we journal with awareness of God's presence with us and with the intention of opening ourselves to hear what God is saying or doing in our lives, journaling becomes profoundly prayerful. It can, however, be hard to know where to begin. The answer is not to overthink but simply to make a start and see what happens. The following exercise uses free writing as an entryway to journaling as a prayerful practice.[11]

Practising
~ You may find it easier to journal after a period of doing something that helps to relax you or breaks any stuck patterns of thinking. You might like to begin with a time of silence or music or physical exercise, such as walking, jogging or swimming.

~ Acknowledge your intent and willingness to be honest about whatever is happening in you and your life. Affirm to yourself that writing a truthful account of how things are with you is a

---

[10] Helen Cepero, *Journaling as a Spiritual Practice* (Downers Grove: InterVarsity Press, 2008), 21.
[11] If you enjoy this, you may like to explore the many other journalling practices and prompts offered by Cepero in *Journaling as a Spiritual Practice*.

practice in telling your story to God. If any of this is difficult, ask for the grace you need.

~ Put the date at the top of your paper.

~ Set a timer for 10 minutes.

~ Write the first thing that comes into your head and keep going.

~ If you can't think of anything to write, write about that.

~ If you find it difficult to write in sentences, write in lists or in clusters.

~ Don't stop writing. If you need to repeat words, that's ok. If you need to write about how much you hate writing, that's ok.

~ Don't cross out mistakes and don't worry about punctuation or grammar. Let yourself lose control and express whatever is asking to be put on the page. If you write something that surprises or shocks you, go with it as it likely has something important to tell you.

~ If you feel really stuck, Helen Cepero recommends beginning with the words "I remember" and then writing for five minutes before turning to a new page and, beginning with the words "I don't remember", writing again for five minutes.

~ If you have a loud inner critic, try writing with your non-dominant hand as a way to interrupt its narrative by deliberately making your writing slower, less legible. You will have to expend more effort actually writing and will have less capacity to critique what you are writing.

~ When you finish, you may like to re-read what you have written and offer it as an honest prayer. If you feel led, dialogue with God about anything you notice as you read.

~ Close the journal and rest your hand on it for a moment as a sign that you are a work in progress and that your story is held and enfolded by God.

PRAYING WITH YOUR MANY PARTS

In *Praying with Body and Soul*, Jane Vennard invites us to consider that we are made up of many parts, acquired over our lifetime in our various roles, emotional states and reactions. These different parts are even more numerous than the different names by which we are called. She writes:

> "Sometimes I am like a wise old woman; sometimes, like a mischievous young boy. I can think and feel and act from my competitive part, or my judgmental part, or my self-righteous part. Many situations bring out the mother in me, but when I am sick I behave like a young and fretful child. Within my identity I have both a cowardly lion and the goddess Artemis, protector of young women. Sometimes I am the rabbit of Alice in Wonderland, running frantically about, shouting, 'I'm late! I'm late!" I am a dancer and a poet, a contemplative and a dreamer, a sadly wounded child."[12]

---

[12] Jane Vennard, *Praying with Body and Soul: A Way to Intimacy with God* (Minneapolis: Augsburg, 1998), 91.

This practice is adapted from one of Vennard's and invites you to pray with the story of your life by becoming aware of different parts of yourself and what they want to say to you and to God. It uses the imagination as a tool to create a safe space for different parts of you, including hidden or repressed parts, to be seen and heard as they express themselves and let you know what they know or need. This can help you to bring more of yourself in prayer and can pave a way towards integration and healing. If this feels strange or unfamiliar, go slowly and be gentle with yourself. If you aren't able to complete the practice, it's worth taking a break and trying again later, perhaps at a different time or in a different place, where you feel safer or more comfortable.

Practising

~ Find a safe or comfortable place where you won't be disturbed for 15-20 minutes.

~ You will be exploring some of your many parts through your imagination so notice how this makes you feel. Are you excited? Nervous? Unsure? Ask for God's blessing on your imagination. Ask that you might be open to seeing and hearing the parts of you that are asking to be seen or heard. Ask for any other favour you need to begin.

~ Imagine you are in a theatre, all by yourself, in a comfortable seat, centre of the front row. You are here not to see a play or a musical but to see some of the many parts of who you are up on the stage. Let the scene unfold around you. Take your time and try not to force it. You may like to name inwardly what you can see, feel, hear or smell.

~ Imagine that some of your many parts are currently hidden behind the curtain and invite them to present themselves, one at a time.

~ Let the curtain go up and wait for some of your parts to appear, one at a time. Notice their movements as they come on stage. What are they wearing? How do they hold their bodies? How do they name themselves? You will probably see some of your most familiar parts, but some new part might reveal itself.

~ Some of your parts may worry or frighten you while others may amuse or delight you. Some of your parts may present themselves as animals or objects. Notice your reaction to your parts but try to resist any urge to analyse what is happening. See if you can remain open to simply seeing what or who appears without trying to label them as "good" or "bad", "acceptable" or "unacceptable". As Vennard writes, "Each part of ourselves offers a gift to the whole of who we are, even if we are not yet clear what the gift might be."[13]

~ If one part seems particularly to draw your attention, you might choose to get to know it better and ask that part what it might want to say to you and to God.

~ Ask it to step forward and tell you its name. Ask what it thinks about and how it feels. Ask what it wants and needs from you. Then ask how it experiences God and how it prays.

~ Listen for the answers and see what you might learn about yourself and your options for prayer. As Vennard explains, "Each of our many parts has a preferred style. The poet in me likes to craft beautiful phrases....the dancer never speaks her prayers; she simply moves...the contemplative longs for quiet and stillness...the wounded child reaches for crayons and draws her prayers."[14] See if this part of you wants to offer a prayer and let it guide you in prayer.

---

[13] Ibid., 93
[14] Ibid., 93.

~ Let the curtain come down on the stage and gently release the scene.

~ Reflect on what you experienced. What was it like to encounter this part? What did it want you to know? How do you want to respond? Express your thoughts and feelings freely to God, in whatever way seems natural and right to you.

Praying with and for Others

In 2014, my dear friend John was killed in a car crash. He was 35. In our last exchange of messages, we shared what was making us happy.

"The sun makes me happy," he wrote, "and lovely people, and Church and wine and theology."

John was intellectually brilliant, a renowned theologian and beloved Dean and Chaplain of Jesus College, Cambridge but it was his childlike joy and gift for seeing the best in people that I valued most about him. We had been particularly close during our time studying together at Cambridge, but we remained good friends, mainly thanks to his faithful and persistent efforts to keep in touch. We had been planning to meet up in just a couple of weeks. The news of his death snatched away my breath; the shock was almost paralysing. After the shock came a tsunami of emotion. I couldn't formulate thoughts; there were no words. I didn't know how to think or what to ask or what to do but I did know where I needed to be: Cambridge.

"I need to be with people who knew and loved John," I told my husband.

The next day I boarded a bus and spent the day walking familiar streets and laying flowers with those also grieving the loss of John. Another friend of John's had arranged a vigil and although I wept a flood of tears, there was comfort in turning to one another and together to God with our unspoken question: "Why?" As we sang and prayed, our voices and tears mingled in one collective lament for our friend.

The shortest verse in the Bible is "Jesus wept." It appears in John's Gospel following the death of Lazarus.[1] Jesus knew death wasn't the end for Lazarus, yet he still wept with those who loved

---

[1] See John 11:35.

153

him. It reminds me that in making all things new, God doesn't dismiss or trivialise our losses and suffering but meets us in our pain and grief as a friend who weeps and laments with us. In that church on that day and with those people, I sensed Jesus weeping with us. I could, of course, have stayed at home and prayed for John alone. But that day I needed to pray with others. In the following days, months and even years, I would return to that experience of collective prayer and remember I was not alone in my grief—John was beloved by his friends and by Jesus, his truest friend who knew best his love of the sun, church, lovely people, wine and theology.

This is just one example of the way in which praying with others grounds us in community, reminding us that we share concerns, hopes, longings, and fears. We come before God not only as individuals but as a people and God responds to us as both individuals and as a people. When it's hard to pray alone, we can draw strength from the experience of corporate prayer, feeling ourselves carried by the prayers of others. This corporate prayer can take many forms, and each has its own beauty and value. For me the rhythm of liturgical prayer is stabilising; the interplay of music and silence in Taizé prayer is restful; the authenticity of spontaneous prayer is encouraging. In all these forms of corporate prayer and more, what is common is the joining of individual voices and hearts in one shared prayer to God.

We come before God not only as individuals but as a people and God responds to us as both individuals and as a people.

Praying for others also grounds community by anchoring each other in love. In his letters to the persecuted early Christian communities, St Paul offers his prayers and asks others to pray for him as well as one another, not so that life will go smoothly or be easy but because prayer grows community by firmly grounding each person in the abundance of Christ's love.[2] This love is wider and deeper and higher and longer than any created phenomenon and prayer is what anchors us within it and bonds us to each other.

It's the connection between prayer and love which, I think, at least partly explains why even those who do not usually think of themselves as pray-ers will respond to tragedy with the words "I'll pray for you." Sometimes people are frustrated by this, viewing this four-word sentence as an empty platitude offered blithely instead of more costly, concrete action. But, when they are offered authentically and with the right intention, those four words can be a great gift: another way of saying "I love you", "God loves you", and "This matters." Understood through this lens, praying for others is not so much telling God about the concerns of another (as though God didn't already know) but of affirming that these concerns are God's concerns, that God knows and loves this person. By praying for others, we align ourselves with God's heart and ground ourselves in awareness of God's love those for whom we pray.

If, though, we're praying for a situation we desperately want to see fixed we can become preoccupied with trying to work out exactly what we want to happen and exactly what we should ask for. In my experience, this is well intentioned and flows from our desire to care for others as best we can but taking responsibility for determining an ideal response is unnecessary. Prayer is not a magic trick. God doesn't respond because we ask for the right things, God responds because in praying we create another opening for love. And, in creating that opening, God's response often comes through us, prompting us to action and moving our prayer into service.

Action and prayer are, then, not separate. Praying for others and serving others are not opposed alternatives but open onto each other. Our prayer is hollow if we treat it as a convenient way of delegating responsibility. God doesn't only work through miracles but through those who love God and those made in God's image. And yet we also need prayer to prevent us from believing that we are

---

[2] See Romans 1:8-10, 2 Corinthians 1:3-7, Ephesians 1:15-23, 2 Thessalonians 3:1, and Colossians 4:2-4.

It is, of course, possible that those who trouble us have hurt us very badly and in these cases we must go especially gently, seeking

By learning to pray for those who trouble us, we leave no part of our lives hidden from the transforming power of God's love.

the deep healing for our inner wounds that we need in order to extend prayer and forgiveness. While some may experience this healing quickly, and find they can quickly offer heartfelt prayer and forgiveness, for others it is a slow, undulating or stop-start process. Both are faithful responses to Jesus' command. What is important is not that we rush to the end but that we remain honest in prayer, leaning into God for the help we need, trusting that God knows our tender places and our struggles. As Flora Slosson Wuellner writes, it is very important that we respect our inner defences and those of others:

> "Never forcibly assault your inner defences and never allow anyone else to do so! That is not the way the Holy Spirit works. And those who come to you truly through the Holy Spirit will not assault your defences. God through Christ respects and has compassion on your inner defences. They will be healed, you will outgrow them, but within the timing and context of God's grace."[6]

This chapter contains practices that invite you to receive other human beings as both a focus for your prayers and your companions in prayer. A few of these practices centre on group prayer and I hope that these ways of praying might suggest some alternatives to the "pass the prayer around the table" model of group prayer or lengthy prepared in advance prayers.

Most of the practices, however, are primarily directed towards use in private prayer, although they could be adapted to use in small

[6] Flora Slosson Wuellner, *Prayer, Stress and Our Inner Wounds* (Nashville: Upper Room Books, 1985), 55.

groups. Perhaps it seems strange to think of private prayer as praying *with*, as well as *for*, others but in a very real and deep sense, you are always praying with others, even when you're alone. Though our prayers are many, they are all connected because they are all expressions of our corporate response to God.

Although I hope these practices offer some fresh ways to pray with and for others, it's important that you approach praying for others in the same freedom as you approach all of prayer. You can use your own words, borrow the words of others or let go of words altogether. You can use your body, your imagination, your intellect, your creativity. Come as yourself, bring what you have and trust that all your movements towards relationship to God are delightful to God.

For reflection

In what ways are you aware of others when you pray?

What is the connection between prayer and service in your life?

Who do you tend to pray for? Who do you tend not to pray for?

THREE WAYS TO PRAY AS A GROUP

There are as many ways to pray with others as there are to pray alone. Often, though, group prayer reverts to a rote pattern. The pattern of this group prayer differs between denominations and depending on group sizes and this isn't problematic except insofar as it might encourage those involved to believe that this is how group prayer should or must look. The following are some suggestions for alternative ways of praying together in a group.

Practising

A. *Silent Prayer*

~ If possible, arrange for people to sit in a circle, either on chairs or on the floor, perhaps on yoga mats.

~ Begin by lighting a candle to remind everyone that Christ is present, perhaps underlining this with reference to a short Biblical passage: for example, Matthew 1:23, Matthew 18:20, Matthew 28:20, or Hebrews 13:8.

~ If silent prayer is unfamiliar to those gathered, a short explanation is helpful. The leader could stress that the silence is already full and that there is nothing to do but rest in it. While some people may notice images or thoughts forming and receive these as gifts from God, these are not the goal of silent, listening prayer. Sometimes our listening takes the form of waiting on God and sometimes what we hear from God reaches deeper places than those of which we are conscious. It's also helpful to offer a word or two about distractions. These distractions are to be expected and can be treated gently by lovingly releasing them when they are noticed; any attempt to rid ourselves of distractions will only result in more appearing.

~ Explain how long the silence will last and how it will be opened and closed. This opening and closing could be a spoken word (for example, "Let us pray"/"Amen") or a chime or other sound.

~ Invite people to find a supportive, comfortable position that they can maintain for the duration of the silence. If sitting, encourage people to uncross their legs and ground their feet on the floor, to straighten their backs, lengthen their necks and place their hands either palm up or palm down on their knees. If lying, encourage people to adopt a savasana position, on their backs, with feet hip distance apart and arms resting on either side.

~ Begin the silence in the agreed way.

~ After the period of silence, you may like to offer a spoken prayer or blessing.

~ In order to allow time for people to linger in the stillness, ask people who wish to speak to move away from the circle.

~ You may like to offer some reflection questions afterwards, either for journaling or for group discussion. For example: how was it to sit/lie in silence? How would you describe the quality of the silence? How did you respond to distractions? Where was your attention? What did you notice afterwards?

B. Repeated Prayer
~ Choose a short prayer or phrase to serve as the repeated prayer. Suggestions include petitions from the Lord's Prayer, verses from the psalms or a simple phrase such as "mend our world," or "love: cast out fear."

~ Seat people in a circle or in another arrangement that allows for an easy flow around the group. Explain that instead of repeating the prayer in unison or passing a turn to pray spontaneously around the group, this petition or phrase will be repeated around the circle. This is intended to allow each person to offer the prayer as their own and to deepen the prayerful meditation of the group.

~ Decide who will begin and which direction the prayer will move. Explain that there is no rush to move the prayer around the group and that the silence between repetitions is as prayerful as the words that are spoken. Invite people to let the silence deepen the prayerful meditation on the repeated phrase.

~ Let the prayer move around the group.

~ Once each person has spoken the phrase, hold a minute or two of silence before saying "Amen."

C. Deep Listening Prayer
~ Arrange chairs in a circle or in another shape that allows everyone to see each other.

~ Begin by explaining that the intention of this time of listening is to help each person to offer to God whatever is happening in their lives or is on their minds or hearts. Explain that, instead of treating a person's story as a precursor to prayer, the group will be offering its collective willingness to be present to each story as their prayer. Emphasise that the listeners are there to hold open a safe space in which the speaker can share their story and to surround them with silent, loving prayer as they do so. Reassure the group that they are not required to respond to what is shared except with their willingness to stay present and attentive.

~ Begin with a minute of silence to ground the group in awareness of the presence of God and then invite each person to briefly share a story or memory. Suggested prompts include: "What word or image describes where you are in life at this moment?", or "What do you want God to do for you?", or "When have you experienced God's presence today/this week/this month?"

~ After each time of listening, thank the speaker and hold a minute of silence to honour them and what they have shared. During this silence, the group are welcome to pray silently for the speaker however they feel led (for example, through silent dialogue with God, by visualising the person held by love, or by inwardly repeating a simple phrase such as "Lord, hear her prayer").

~ Close the time together with a spoken prayer or blessing or with more silence.

PRAYING THE PRAYERS OF OTHERS

One way to become more intentional about praying with others is through joining the prayers of others, offering their words as our words. By doing this we connect ourselves with the broader praying church across history and time. There can also be freedom in releasing the belief that we must be original in prayer in order for it to be authentic and meaningful. Sometimes praying words that have first been written or spoken by another frees us from self-consciousness or self-criticism and assists us in praying from a place deeper within. What matters is not that the words are fresh but that they are spoken from the heart.

Practising

~ Decide which prayer you will offer as your own. Below is a small selection of prayers from well-known Christians across the ages. They have already been prayed with and by others over years, sometimes centuries.

~ Consider praying these out loud or by copying them out in your own handwriting. You could take a line or phrase and use it as a starting point for your own prayer.

~ End your prayer time with a moment of silence to allow the words to settle deeper and for your heart to silently commune with or rest in God.

∞

O Lord my God,
Teach my heart this day where and how to see you,
Where and how to find you.
You have made me and remade me,
And you have bestowed on me
All the good things I possess,
And still I do not know you.
I have not yet done that
For which I was made.
Teach me to seek you,
For I cannot seek you
Unless you teach me,
Or find you
Unless you show yourself to me.
Let me seek you in my desire,

Let me desire you in my seeking.
Let me find you by loving you,
Let me love you when I find you.
~ Saint Anselm (1033-1109)[7]

∞

Lord, make me an instrument of your peace.
Where there is hatred, let me bring love.
Where there is offence, let me bring pardon.
Where there is discord, let me bring union.
Where there is error, let me bring truth.
Where there is doubt, let me bring faith.
Where there is despair, let me bring hope.
Where there is darkness, let me bring your light.
Where there is sadness, let me bring joy.
O Master, let me not seek as much
to be consoled as to console,
to be understood as to understand,
to be loved as to love,
for it is in giving that one receives,
it is in self-forgetting that one finds,
it is in pardoning that one is pardoned,
it is in dying that one is raised to eternal life.
~ Attributed to St Francis of Assisi (1181-1226)[8]

∞

Let nothing disturb you,
Let nothing frighten you,

---

[7] As quoted at https://acollectionofprayers.com/2016/06/20/a-prayer-of-st-anselm/   (accessed 4 April, 2022).
[8] As quoted at https://www.lords-prayer-words.com/famous_prayers/make_me_a_channel_of_your_peace_lyrics.html (accessed 4 April, 2022).

All things pass away:
God never changes.
Patience obtains all things
They who have God lack nothing;
God alone is enough.
~ St Teresa of Avila (1515-1582)[9]

∞

Dear Jesus, help us to spread Your fragrance
    everywhere we go.
Flood our souls with Your Spirit and Life.
Penetrate and possess our whole being so utterly
    that our lives may only be a radiance of Yours.
Shine through us and be so in us
    that every soul we come in contact with may feel
        Your presence in our souls.
Let them look up, and see no longer us, but only
    Jesus!
Stay with us and then we shall begin to shine as You
    shine,
    so to shine as to be a light to others.
The light, O Jesus, will be all from You; none of it
    will be ours.
It will be You, shining on others through us.
Let us thus praise You in the way You love best, by
    shining on those around us.
Let us preach You without preaching, not by words
    but by example,
    by the catching force, the sympathetic influence of
    what we do,

---

[9] As quoted at https://carmelite.com/let-nothing-disturb-you/ (accessed 4 April, 2022).

the evident fullness of the love our hearts bear for
You. Amen.

~ John Henry Newman (1801-1890),
a favourite prayer of Mother Teresa[10]

∞

Disturb us, O Lord,
when we are too well-pleased with ourselves,
when our dreams have come true because we
dreamed too little,
because we sailed too close to the shore.
Disturb us, O Lord,
when with the abundance of things we possess,
we have lost our thirst for the water of life
when, having fallen in love with time,
we have ceased to dream of eternity
and in our efforts to build a new earth,
we have allowed our vision of Heaven to grow dim.
Stir us, O Lord
to dare more boldly, to venture into wider seas
where storms show Thy mastery,
where losing sight of land, we shall find the stars.
In the name of Him who pushed back the horizons
of our hopes and invited the brave to follow.
Amen.

~ Attributed to Archbishop Desmond Tutu (1931-
2021)[11]

---

[10] As quoted by Mother Teresa in *No Greater Love* (Novato: New World Library,
1989), 158.
[11] As quoted at https://godspacelight.com/2012/03/02/disturb-us-o-lord-a-prayer-
by-desmond-tutu-4/ (accessed 4 April, 2022)

MAP PRAYER

Visual prompts can be helpful in guiding our prayer for other people, especially those who live far away. This practice suggests a way to use a map as a prompt for intercessory prayer.

Practising

~ Put up a map of the world in your home or room as a reminder that our human community is global. If you feel drawn to pray for places closer to home, you may also like to display a map of your country or town.

~ Each day or week choose a country or city and pray for it. You may like to use words or you may want to simply soften your gaze as you allow your love, attention and presence to become focused on that place on the map. Alternatively, you may like to place a hand gently on that place, as a sign of your intention to join God in blessing that place. You might begin with places you have visited, or places where you have friends or family. You might also allow news stories to guide you in which countries to pray for. Many Christian agencies offer resources to guide prayers for its work. For example, World Vision offers a monthly email for anyone who wishes to join its Hope Prayer Team.

~ In addition to praying for the place with words, gaze or touch, you may also like to reflect on whether there's a tangible way in which you might bless or honour that place and its people, perhaps through a charitable donation or by joining a campaign or by raising awareness of its needs with your friends and family.

NEWS STORY PRAYER

Most of us are bombarded with information about the world and it can leave us feeling overwhelmed and unsure how to respond. Slowing down our reading and learning to take time to sit with those stories that seem particularly significant can be a deeply prayerful way of interrupting any tendency to want to accrue information for its own sake. While wanting to be informed is understandable, approaching the news as a gateway to prayer may help you to develop a deeper, more spiritually engaged response to what you discover.

Practising

~ Look through a print or online newspaper and let your attention settle on one particular issue or event. Bring it with you to a quiet place where you can pray or place it somewhere you will see it during the day.

~ Ask God to open your mind and heart and to give you the courage to go deeper into the situation or issue so that you may more fully pray for it. Who is affected or involved? Use your imagination to enter into the situation or consider the issue.

~ Imagine being a person directly involved. If you are involved, imagine being someone else who is involved. Explore different perspectives, noticing how you respond. Ask yourself:

> *Who do I most easily empathise with?*
> *Who do I find it hardest to empathise with?*
> *What would justice look like in this situation or issue?*
> *What would mercy look like?*
> *How does this situation or issue connect with others?*
> *Do any passages or stories or images from Scripture come to mind?*

How might I respond, in practical ways, to this situation or issue?

~ Ask these questions slowly and take time to listen. Prepare to be unsettled or surprised by what may come to the surface. Hold what comes lightly, noticing any tendency towards judgement or condemnation of yourself or others.

~ Gather your thoughts into a prayer to God but know that your whole time of reflection has been prayerful because you began by opening your heart and mind to God. Slow down your prayer, offering up your honest reflections, feelings and desires.

~ Take time to listen to how God might be stirring you to respond in thought, or word or action. Even after you end your prayer, be attentive to the Spirit's guidance with this issue or situation during the rest of the day.

PRAYING FOR THOSE WHO TROUBLE US

Jesus tells us to love our enemies and pray for those who persecute us but before we can do this we need to recognise who these people are. This prayer intends to help you with identifying those challenging people or groups and offers a gentle pathway towards release and healing. Go slowly and be gentle with yourself if you experience any resistance.

Practising
~ Ask yourself these questions and try to be as honest as possible:
Who do I resent?

Who do I struggle to love?
To whom am I ideologically opposed?
For whom do I not pray?

~ Gather together these names or faces.

~ Picture the light of God or the arms of Jesus or another image that, for you, represents God's love.

~ Imagine placing the names or faces in that space of love. If you find this difficult, it may help to imagine the hurt, frightened, lonely or bewildered child in the other person and visualise that part being handed over, enfolded or embraced by God's love.

~ Picture also your pain, resentment and feelings of hurt, anger or hate being handed over. This will likely be difficult, perhaps extremely so. Offer as much as you can but do not feel ashamed if you are unable to do this in one sitting.

~ If you can, imagine yourself receiving back from God peace, trust, and love. Even if you do not feel these things, see if you can trust that they are offered to you. By releasing, or attempting to release, fear and anger and pain, you are opening yourself to receiving God's gifts more fully. God will hold these people and feelings for you. In time, they will be transformed according to God's perfect love, which includes justice as well as mercy, just as you also are being transformed through love.

~ End by resting quietly in the image of God's love as it came to you.

DOORWAY PRAYER

Praying for others and serving others are inextricably linked. Without embodied action, our prayer for others is incomplete and without prayer we can become disillusioned, burnt out or smugly self-satisfied. One way to encourage a healthy flow between prayer and action is to turn the threshold times in our days into prayerful times. By "threshold times" I mean those times when we are stepping out of our homes or familiar spaces into new spaces and community with others.

Even if you find yourself rushing in and out of your house, you might find that you can incorporate a brief version of this practice into your daily routine. Feel free to play with the words associated with each of the inhales and exhales; simply ask for the blessings you desire to receive and to give.

Practising
~ Before leaving your home or at the beginning of the day allow yourself a few moments to pause before leaving the house.

~ Quietly observe your thoughts and feelings. Are you excited? Stressed? Anxious?

~ Take some deep breaths, silently repeating the following words:
Inhale: *I breathe in the blessing of God.*
Exhale: *So that I may offer blessing to others.*

~ You may also like to offer a short prayer, for example:
Loving God, I can only give what I have received. Help me to let go of what prevents me from receiving your love. Help me to leave behind my judgement, my suspicion, my fear. Open my eyes to see those you want me to see and embolden me to respond with love. Amen.

~ On returning to your home or at the end of the day, allow yourself a few moments to pause.

~ Allow your mind to wander over your day. Which encounters stand out? What thoughts and feelings do you notice?

~ Ask yourself: when did I see the image of God in others today? When did I struggle to see God in others today?

~ Take some deep breaths, silently repeating the following words:
Inhale: *I soak in the peace of Christ.*
Exhale: *May peace be upon all people.*

~ You may like to end with this prayer, or similar:
Loving God, I thank you for being with me today. For those times I saw your image in other people, thank you. For the times I struggled to see you, forgive me. Perfect me in your love. Grant me rest that I may be refreshed to see you in all people. Amen.

Praying with Our Imaginations

A few years ago I had an experience of God's love that turned my life upside down. It came during a period of inner wrestling that was honest, painful, and deeply prayerful. Every afternoon while my children napped, I would retreat to my bedroom and let everything I was holding inside pour out. There was no particular pattern or method except beginning with the words "Here I am." One day, after months of this, I sensed an invitation to go into our living room and sit on the couch.

"Don't be afraid," a soft, inward voice whispered. "I am here. Bring it all to me."

I followed the instruction and as I inwardly opened my eyes to the complete jumble of heavy feelings, I felt overwhelmed and completely terrified. My fear seemed to be a bottomless pit into which I was falling.

But, right at the moment of greatest terror, love rushed in like a gentle breeze. The fear was gone in an instant. It was effortless and joyful. There was no weight to this love, yet it was incomparably real and substantial.

The experience intensified and as I felt myself enfolded in love, I became aware of arms around me and of a presence holding me. I received this as an angelic presence: not God but *from* God. It was a profoundly healing experience of love casting out fear and the complete trust and openness I felt melted my resistance to receiving it. For months afterwards I experienced a deep centeredness and peace that overflowed into my relationships and seemed to show me the way to go.

If this all sounds crazy, I understand. There was no outward sign or proof and although I had felt the hug, there had been no physical arms. I was sitting on my sofa with my back pressed into the cushions. My awareness of being held by an angelic presence was purely internal, a mysterious knowing that the presence holding me was in some sense a messenger of God, anchoring my embodied self firmly in the love of God.

While the experience facilitated a profound inner shift, I was confused about if or how to speak of it. I knew that something real and significant had happened but wondered if it would be viewed as all in my head, a figment of my imagination.

When I shared my experience with a trusted friend, he listened attentively. After a while I asked him what he thought had happened and held my breath as I waited for his response.

He took some time to reflect and then quietly offered: "Was it psychological? Yes. Can God work through our psyches and our imaginations? Yes, absolutely."

Initially, I felt deflated. Hadn't my friend just told me it was all in my head? But then I heard the truth in his words. Just because I had experienced God's love through the working of my imagination it didn't mean I hadn't experienced God. There was no contradiction between the experience being "in my imagination" and "from God"; both were true. If God created the imagination, God could work through it and, while I had no proof that this is what had happened, the positive, life-giving trajectory this experience had set me on was evidence enough for me that something sacred had happened. As Jesus teaches, it is our fruit that reveals the truth about us and our experiences, far more than their specific details.[1]

Perhaps you find it difficult to receive your imagination as a conduit of spiritual healing or to trust it in any deep sense. This is hardly surprising. Most of us are used to opposing the imaginary to the real and, thinking that our imaginations deceive us, tend to treat them with suspicion. We may think that entering into our imaginations means leaving reality and separating ourselves from others, or that embracing our imaginations encourages a dangerous individualism or subjectivism. Perhaps we worry that if we allow

---

[1] Matthew 7:15-20.

ourselves to enter the realm of imagination we will never return to the real world. These are understandable concerns but ones that are rooted in a false dualism between imagination and reality. Yes, our imaginations can be used as a way of avoiding or escaping our embodied life or the facts of the world as it is, but this is a misuse of imagination. Used properly, our imaginations help us to go beneath the surface of our experience, allowing us to see deeper truths about the world, ourselves, others, and God. They help us to receive—and to keep receiving—what is given. Through imagination and its closely allied companion, memory, we enter and re-enter our experiences, weaving together these experiences and drawing meaning from them.

> *Our imaginations help us to go beneath the surface of our experience, allowing us to see deeper truths about the world, ourselves, others, and God.*

Take the example of a rose. While our senses facilitate an embodied experience and our brains provide understanding, it's our capacity to imagine and remember that allow us to join together discrete encounters, to connect them with other moments of beauty, and to draw meaning from them. Without imagination there would be no poetry about roses, no association with love, no bouquets of roses at weddings.

One of my greatest teachers in the importance and value of imagination is herself imaginary: the heroine of L. M. Montgomery's *Anne of Green Gables*.

Anne is an orphan who has lived a hard life with her imagination as her only consolation. At 11 she is delighted to be adopted. It turns out that it was a mistake; middle aged siblings Matthew and Marilla Cuthbert had wanted a boy to help on the farm. After glimpsing the unkindness with which she has been treated at the orphanage, they decide to keep her anyway. Anne is awkward, outspoken, and accident prone but she is also sensitive, intelligent, and creative.

Matthew is pleasantly perplexed by Anne but Marilla disapproves of her flighty ways and her overactive imagination.

It's true that Anne sometimes uses her imagination as an escape or coping mechanism, a way of avoiding or managing reality. It's also true that her imaginings lead her into scrapes, such as when she is picturing herself as "a Catholic – taking the veil to bury a broken heart in cloistered seclusion" and she forgets to cover the plum pudding, resulting in a mouse sneaking in for a taste and drowning in the sauce.[2] But her imagination is also her greatest gift. Not only does it console her, but it also helps her to be more present to the world around her, to draw out its beauty and possibility and to see more deeply.

"'Aren't those gulls splendid? Would you like to be a gull? I think I would—that is, if I couldn't be a human girl. Don't you think it would be nice to wake up at sunrise and swoop down over the water and away out over that lovely blue all day; and then at night to fly back to one's nest? Oh, I can just imagine myself doing it."[3]

As a child reading the books, I received Anne as a teacher of both imagination and joy. Anne helped me to enjoy the tree I could see from my bedroom window, she encouraged me to examine bark and make dens in hidden spots in the garden. As an adult reader, I also receive Anne as a spiritual teacher with an intuition about what is important in prayer. She recognises that "saying one's prayers isn't exactly the same thing as praying,"[4] echoing Jesus' parable of the Pharisee and the tax collector,[5] and she understands that prayer doesn't need to be complicated or eloquent—a surprise considering she is usually so attracted to flowery language. "I just said 'Thank you for it, God, two or three times,"[6] she explains to Marilla. Such gratitude is a cornerstone of her prayers, and they often flow from her wonder at and enjoyment of nature.

---

[2] L. M. Montgomery, *Anne of Green Gables* (New York: Barnes and Noble, 2016), 151.

[3] Ibid., 50.

[4] Ibid., 91.

[5] See Luke 18:9-14.

[6] L. M. Montgomery, *Anne of Green Gables* (New York: Barnes and Noble), 2016, 97.

Anne also intuitively knows how imagination can become a spiritual practice. Consider this passage taken from near the beginning of the book in which Marilla asks Anne what she's staring at:

> "'That,' she said, pointing to the picture – a rather vivid chromo entitled 'Christ Blessing Little Children'—'and I was just imagining I was one of them—that I was the little girl in the blue dress, standing off by herself in the corner as if she didn't belong to anybody, like me. She looks lonely and sad, don't you think? I guess she hadn't any father or mother of her own. But she wanted to be blessed, too, so she just crept shyly up on the outside of the crowd, hoping nobody would notice her—except Him. I'm sure I know just how she felt. Her heart must have beat and her hands must have gone cold, like mine did when I asked you if I could stay. She was afraid He mightn't notice her. But it's likely He did, don't you think? I've been trying to imagine it all out—her edging a little nearer all the time until she was quite close to Him; and then He would look at her and put His hand on her hair and oh, such a thrill of joy as would run over her!'"[7]

Unsurprisingly, Marilla is shocked by this imagining, calling it "positively irreverent" and telling Anne "it doesn't sound right to talk so familiarly about such things."[8] Yet, while Marilla is unimpressed by Anne's imaginative response to the picture, any Jesuit would be very impressed, indeed. Anne's use of her imagination to enter into the gospel scene depicted in the chromo is akin to what St Ignatius encouraged in his Spiritual Exercises, and

---

[7] Ibid., 67.
[8] Ibid., 67.

if it sounds familiar to you, it may well be because it is very similar to the Gospel contemplation practice outlined in the first chapter.

In many ways, St Ignatius has nurtured my adult self as Anne nurtured my childhood self. Like Anne, St Ignatius was also given to flights of fancy and treasured imagination, feeling and gratitude. Recovering from surgery following the battle of Pamplona in 1521, he had only two books for company: one was a collection of stories about the saints, and the other a volume about the life of Christ, *De Vita Christi* by Ludolph of Saxony. These books were in stark contrast to the books about knights and maidens that he ordinarily chose to read but, because he had nothing else to read, he opened them and stepped into a process of inner awakening. As he lay in bed in pain, he oscillated from fantasising about being a knight winning the affection of a young lady to imagining himself a saint, doing great things for God and God's people. Gradually he noticed that, while both felt good in the moment, the feelings lasted longer with his saintly imaginings than with winning the heart of a maiden. This began a discernment process that led him to dedicate his life to God and found the Jesuit order.

Becoming aware of the imagination's ability to be a pathway into the interior also alerted Ignatius to the broad value of the imagination in the spiritual life as a way of both exploring and receiving God's Word and presence. Ignatius knew that, while it is possible to hide from God in imagination, it can also be the place where we meet God most intimately and can become the key to the flourishing of our faith. As David Fleming S.J. explains, imaginative prayer makes the Jesus of the Gospels personal by helping us to place ourselves directly in relationship with him. Jesus is no longer bound within the pages of Scripture or confined to the cloisters of tradition but is revealed as our Jesus who speaks to the circumstances of our unique and messy lives.[9] This isn't selfish or egocentric, but necessary for spiritual growth and flourishing.

---

[9] "[Imaginative prayer] allows the person of Christ to penetrate into places that the intellect does not touch. It brings Jesus into our hearts. It engages our feelings. It enflames us with ideals of generous service." David Fleming, *What is Ignatian Spirituality?* (Chicago: Loyola Press, 2008), 58.

To pray with our imaginations, then, means to be open both to expressing ourselves to God with creative and playful thought and to hearing God speak to or move us in new and perhaps surprising ways. It means affirming our inner world as a place of encounter with God.

To begin with, praying with our imaginations can feel alien and perhaps even dangerous. If we're used to prayer as very earnest or following a prescribed pattern of formula it can feel like free-falling. Praying with imagination requires a willingness to be playful and experimental. It requires us to believe that our dreaming need not take us away from God but can be revealing and can help us to discern our hopes and joys. It can deepen our awareness of God's presence in our world. This approach isn't unscriptural and not only because we're taught to love God with our whole selves, imagination included. In both Old and New Testaments, God speaks to people through dreams and Jesus used imaginative story-telling methods to teach the crowds. Many times over, Scripture encourages us to imagine a different future for ourselves and the world and to allow this to shape and fuel our work. At its best, imagination feeds hope, nurtures our creativity, and strengthens community.

To pray with our imaginations means affirming our inner world as a place of encounter with God.

And yet Scripture also warns of the dangers of imagination, both for how we approach God and for how we treat each other. The commandment against making images of God is a warning about becoming satisfied with our own, limited imaginings. We can't picture God because our imaginations are insufficient for the task. This also applies to petitionary prayer since our limited imaginations can lead us to set limits on what we ask for from God, when in reality God can do "immeasurably more than all we ask or imagine." Jesus' teaching about adultery beginning in the heart makes it clear that imagination also has dangers for our relationships with others. Imagination is not always a neutral space and the hurt we inflict on each other and ourselves often begins in our imaginings. St. Paul echoes this when he indicates that we can easily become self-centred and vain through overindulging our imaginations. While imagination has the capacity to transcend rigidity, deepen compassion and draw us closer to God, it also has a tendency to inflate the ego and diminish God's goodness as well as to make us forgetful of our neighbours and our truest selves.

It's important, then, to treat our imaginations with both honour and caution. When praying with our imaginations, it's a good idea to relate any insights to what we already trust to be true of God and ourselves. Some of the images and insights we encounter through praying with our imaginations may be new, perhaps even startlingly so, and this can be both exciting and unsettling. A healthy response to this experience involves holding the middle ground, neither rejecting the new out of hand nor immediately throwing everything familiar away. For this reason, it can be helpful to share our experiences with a spiritual director or a trusted spiritual friend who knows us well and can help us in the work of unpacking experiences and discerning how to respond to them. This doesn't mean that we deny our experiences or neatly slot every encounter into the existing structures of our spiritual lives. Instead, it means focusing on listening to God and remaining open to having our limited perspectives expanded. This takes time and, because a genuine insight from God will keep deepening, we don't need to be in a rush to make sense of it or to respond. If it's a good gift for us it'll root and grow in its due season.

This section contains several practices clustered around the theme of praying with our imaginations. Some take their cue from Scripture, others from images and words. Others begin with reflection on our lives and the questions we have. As always, these are practices to be encountered and not simply read. It's good to be aware of resistance and important to be gentle with resistance, but a playful curiosity goes far in readying us for prayer and spiritual encounter. It's in that spirit that I hope you will receive these practices.

For reflection

How has your imagination been important in your life?

In what ways might your imagination help to deepen your prayer life?

Do you feel any resistance to the idea of using your imagination in prayer?

PRAYING SEATED AT THE FEET OF JESUS

This prayer focuses on one particular scene, taken from the following passage of Luke's Gospel:

> "As Jesus and his disciples were on their way, he came to a village where a woman named Martha opened her home to him. She had a sister called Mary, who sat at the Lord's feet listening to what he said. But Martha was distracted by all the preparations that had to be made. She came to him and asked, 'Lord, don't you care that my sister has left me to do the work by myself? Tell her to help me!'
>
> "'Martha, Martha,' the Lord answered, 'you are worried and upset about many things, but few things are needed—or indeed only one. Mary has chosen what is better, and it will not be taken away from her.'"[10]

Often, we can be like Martha, anxious and distracted. We can struggle to allow ourselves to become still and listen for Jesus's loving voice. The following practice encourages you to use your imagination to help you to enter into Mary's posture of receptive openness, to speak to Jesus and to await a response.

Practising

~ Find a comfortable, quiet space where you won't be disturbed for 15-20 minutes.

~ Begin by taking an honest look at your life as it is now. Which words or images or questions come to mind? Write them down and gently set the paper aside.

---

[10] Luke 10:38-42.

184

~ Imagine that you are seated at Jesus' feet like Mary, the sister of Martha and Lazarus. This is the position of one who wishes to listen and converse calmly, without haste. Mary "sat at the Lord's feet and listened to what he was saying."[11] Notice how you respond to assuming this position? How easily do you settle into it? Does it challenge you in any way? Is there any resistance? Acknowledge what comes but don't try to change it. Let your experience be what it is.

~ Breathe deeply and slowly as you relax, or try to relax, deeper into attentive stillness at Jesus's feet.

~ Remaining seated at Jesus' feet in your imagination, return to the words, images and questions that you wrote down. Bring them to your teacher. How does he respond? Notice his expression, his movements. What does he have to say to you? What feelings or inner movements do you notice?

~ Respond however you feel led. You might want to ask more questions, or you may want to imagine yourself responding in a physical way.

~ Breathe deeply and release the imagined scene and all that has arisen through it. Trust that what is important for your healing and your growth will be remembered and will settle deeper without you having to force it.

---

[11] Luke 10:39.

PRAYER FOR THE FUTURE

The following practice is adapted from an exercise in Flora Slosson Wuellner's *Prayer, Stress and Our Inner Wounds*. It takes its inspiration from Psalm 139 and centres on using our imaginations to visualise Christ's presence with us in upcoming stressful situations. You may find this practice particularly helpful if you are prone to worrying about the future or if there's a particular event that you are dreading.

Practising

~ Begin by reading the whole of Psalm 139 or this short extract:
 "You hem me in, behind and before, and lay your hand
 upon me...Where can I go from your Spirit? Where can
 I flee from your presence? If I go up to the heavens, you
 are there; if I make my bed in the depths, you are there.
 If I rise on the wings of the dawn, if I settle on the far
 side of the sea, even there your hand will guide me,
 your right hand will hold me fast."[12]

~ Relax, close your eyes, and visualise Jesus coming into the room,
 in whatever form is best for you. Be open to being surprised here,
 he may not come in the form you think he should take.

~ Relax and breathe in his presence and light.

~ Together, look at some specific point in the time ahead, at an
 experience to come.

~ Imagine Jesus walking ahead of you in confidence and strength
 and entering the place where that experience will unfold,
 whether that's a business office, a classroom, a doctor's surgery,
 a pulpit, a home, an aeroplane, a committee room or other space.

---

[12] Psalm 139:5-10.

Watch him moving around that place, filling every corner with light, blessing and healing. Notice how he moves and what he does. Pay attention to his hands. How is he preparing this place as a safe space for you?

~ Imagine him now turning to look at you with kindness and gentleness. How does he show you that when you enter that place you will feel his presence, comfort and guidance? Perhaps he smiles or reaches out to you. What does he want you to know?

~ Turn your attention again to the place where you are now and see if you can affirm your trust that the future event is in good hands. If this is difficult, you may like to ask for this trust.

PRAYER FOR YOUR INNER CHILD

We all carry within us at least one part that is particularly vulnerable and that we try to keep hidden. Flora Slosson Wuellner refers to this part as the inner child and in her book *Prayer, Stress and our Inner Wounds* outlines a prayerful pathway towards healing for this vulnerable part. It is important to take this exercise slowly and to listen to your bodily and emotional cues. Praying with your imagination can be deeply healing but it can also be frightening if it brings up experiences or emotions you thought you had left behind or had, perhaps, intentionally buried. If you experience any resistance or fear while praying in this way, don't try to overcome it with force of will. Honour your inner defences as you would honour a hurting child who needs to be given time and space. Instead of forcing yourself on, try to be honest with God about your resistance, fear or pain. This willingness itself is a step along the path towards healing.

Practising
~ Relax your body and gratefully acknowledge that God's love is always present, always embracing you.

~ Picture God's love, perhaps in the form of Jesus, entering the room and filling it with warmth and comfort. He who said "Let the children come to me"[13] now tenderly invites your own "most deeply wounded, problematic self"[14] to come to him. Wuellner explains that this is "the one you have hidden, the one you have hated, the one within who feels the weakest, the ugliest, the most vulnerable, the most shameful, the frightening or the most frightened."[15] Take your time here, be patient with yourself as you wait for your hurting part to come forwards. Let it present itself in whatever form it likes. It may come forwards as a child or it may offer itself in the form of an animal or plant or some other object. Let the experience be what it is.

~ Take a long, loving look at this hurt part. If you have imagined God's love in the form of Jesus, imagine him looking lovingly on the hurt part with you. Notice its form, its expression, its movement. Listen to anything it might like to say.

~ If you feel a desire to move towards your hurting part, perhaps to embrace it, hold it or lift it, you can, but don't force yourself to do this if you don't want to touch it. In time this reluctance will also be healed but, for now, simply speak to God's love about your reluctance.

~ See if you have anything you'd like to say to your hurting part. Wuellner suggests: "I hear you. I didn't realise how badly you

---

[13] Luke 18:16.
[14] Flora Slosson Wuellner, *Prayer, Stress, and Our Inner Wounds* (Nashville: The Upper Room, 1985), 52.
[15] Ibid., 52.

were hurting. You belong to me, but I can't heal you alone. Let's go together to the One who *can* heal."[16]

~ If it feels safe to do so, release your hurting part, your inner child to God's love, however you have imagined it. If you have pictured God's love in the form of Jesus, you may want to place the hurt part into his healing hands. If, however, you find that you can't do this or that your inner hurt part doesn't want to go to those hands, don't force the release. If it feels safer, you could ask Jesus, or God's love in another form, to come to you both, gently surrounding both you and your hurt part. If this doesn't feel safe either, simply allow yourself to be present to your hurt part, with awareness that God's healing love is gently present with you and patiently available to you.

~ If you were able to release the hurt part into God's love, let it be held, comforted as long as it would like. It is being healed and, as Wuellner expresses it, "restored slowly to its original beauty and unique creativity."[17]

~ After a while, it may seem that the hurt part, your inner child, is being restored to you. Or you may, instead, imagine it still being carried in the divine heart of transforming love.

~ Breathe deeply and release the imagined scene and all that has arisen through it. Know that you can return to this practice however many times you like. Trust that the process of healing will continue beneath the level of your conscious awareness.

---

[16] Ibid., 52.
[17] Ibid., 53.

DIALOGUE JOURNALING

If journaling is the practice of expressing ourselves on paper, dialogue journaling is the practice of expressing on paper both ourselves and God's words to us. This practice, inspired by a journaling exercise in Helen Cepero's *Journaling as a Spiritual Practice*, asks that you use your imagination to help you to listen for what God has to say to you or, perhaps more accurately, to playfully explore what God might have to say to you. Because your imagination is involved, you may feel that what you hear can't be from God, but those who try this practice often find that what they hear is so surprisingly insightful and truth-laden that it is difficult not to believe that it is, in some mysterious way, from God.

Practising

~ Agree with yourself how long you will journal. Thankfully acknowledge God's presence with you and affirm your openness to be open and to listen. Also acknowledge that the inner critic and the inner censor will try to convince you that this dialogue cannot happen or, if it does, cannot be true and affirm your intention to ignore them, at least for now, and to have a go anyway.

~ Write your own name in your journal, followed by a colon.

~ Give God an unedited version of how things are with you right now, writing in stream-of-consciousness prose.

~ Now write "God" or "Jesus" or "Holy Spirit" or "Love", followed by a colon.

~ Put down your pen or rest your fingers on the keyboard and listen for a response. This is unlikely to be an audible voice but an inner voice that seems to bubble up to the surface of awareness, perhaps from your heart centre. If you hear nothing or if this seems crazy to you, leave a blank space and, underneath, put your own name again with a colon and write, "This feels crazy" or "I don't hear anything." Don't fill in the blank space next to God's name until you feel led to do so.

~ Journal back and forth between you and God for the length of time you agreed. Even if you are not able to write anything for God, Cepero affirms the importance of listening and that sometimes this opens a conversation that continues later in the day, perhaps even between journaling sessions, and that, eventually, there will be something to put in the space next to God.

~ Try not to give up after just one attempt. Cepero suggests that you try this way of praying for at least a week as an experiment in journal prayer.

PRAYING WITH DREAM IMAGES

The Bible contains many examples of God directly speaking to people during their dreams but, for most of us, our dreams offer wisdom in a more subtle way, offering us insights into our unconscious desires, fears or knowings. Sometimes, the reason for, or meaning of, our dreams is clear, but they often leave us confused. We may intuit that a dream holds significance but struggle to make sense of it. While dream analysis can be a fruitful practice, you don't need to be an expert in order to begin to incorporate dreamwork into your spiritual practice. In *Praying with Body and Soul*, Jane Vennard suggests that when reflecting on dream images, we ask ourselves not "what does this mean?" but "how might this dream guide me in prayer?"[18] This practice builds upon Vennard's invitation and instead of offering a way to analyse or explain your dreams, encourages you to explore how your dream images may be inviting you to pray.

Practising

~ Begin by asking God to illuminate your memory and to guide you as you engage your dream images.

~ Remember a dream that has felt significant or a dream which recurs frequently.

~ Write it down in as much detail as you can, using the following questions to help you. What do you remember as being most significant about the dream? Where was the energy in the dream? Was anything particularly surprising about the dream? How did you feel during the dream? How did you feel afterwards?

~ As you explore these questions, try to maintain an open-handed, curious approach. The aim is not to analyse or even to understand the dream but to re-enter it and to allow it to guide you.

~ How does the dream invite prayer? Is an emotion asking to be expressed? Is a memory asking to be considered? Is there a question that wants to be asked? Allow your responses to guide you in prayer and leave plenty of silent space to notice what happens in response. Try to be open to being surprised by any connections, memories or feelings that may present themselves.

---

[18] Jane Vennard, *Praying with Body and Soul: A Way to Intimacy with God* (Minneapolis: Augsburg, 1998), 85.

~ If you feel resistance to entering the dream or it leaves you feeling fearful, offer that to God. Try to trust in God's gentle nearness and in the slow, ongoing work of grace in your life, both in waking and sleeping.

Praying with Our Creativity

One of my happiest childhood memories is of painting with my grandparents. It was a rainy day and the three of us gathered around their dining room table and busied ourselves with our paper and paints with the falling rain on the conservatory roof providing the background music. I don't remember what I made but I do remember the feeling of togetherness, of being present to each other and to our work. There was a peace, an expansive openness, a sense of possibility and unhurried expectancy. I'd forgotten all about this memory until recently when I was watching my children happily occupied with their paints and was reminded that I, too, had found joy in painting as a child.

Picasso famously said, "Every child is an artist. The problem is how to remain an artist once he grows up."[1] That has proved true for me. It's been hard to rediscover the artist I once was as a child. Since remembering that happy time with my grandparents, I've begun to paint and draw again but it's hard to believe that the art I create matters. I no longer have the unselfconscious joy in making that I had as a child and tend to think that it's a waste of time and that I should be doing something more productive or useful, something where I can be more certain of achieving a specific result. But when I do manage to silence or ignore the inner critic and sit down with paints and pens, something wonderful happens. I become present to colour, line, and shape, and I'm utterly caught up in the process of attending to what is unfolding on the page.

---

[1] As quoted in "Modern Living: Ozmosis in Central Park" from *Time* magazine, 4 October, 1976 (accessed 4 April, 2022 at http://content.time.com/time/subscriber/article/0,33009,918412-1,00.html)

Even when I don't paint, I experience a similar unselfing when writing, when gardening, when baking, when tending spaces to make them welcoming to my family and to others. All these, and more, are creative activities and all are deeply soulful. Not because they're accompanied by deep reflection, or pious thoughts but because through them I become present to Presence, lost in the flow of a creative energy that carries me, at one with the hum of creation itself.

Picasso traces our creativity back to childhood but in the Judeo-Christian tradition our creativity is written into our being, as essential to what it means to be human as our DNA. As Christine Valters Paintner writes:

> "If God is creator, and we are made in God's image or *Imago Dei*, then we are, in our essence, creators. We are, in our essence, artists. Therefore, when we open ourselves to the expression of creativity, we also open to the movement of the Divine within us."[2]

Creativity, for Paintner, isn't a gift that some of us possess and others don't. Instead, it's foundational to what it means to be human. The question is not whether we are creative or not but whether we will open ourselves to expressing our innate creativity. And, as Painter implies, this opening is a sacred act, one through which we become more open to God, the Creator at work within and through us.

The question is not whether we are creative or not but whether we will open ourselves to expressing our innate creativity.

Perhaps it seems strange to think of God as at work through our creativity, perhaps we think of God's creativity and our creativity as operating on separate tracks, with God's creativity very much superior to our own. But, in Genesis, Adam isn't created

[2] Christine Valters Paintner and Betsey Beckman, *Awakening the Creative Spirit: Bringing the Arts to Spiritual Direction* (Harrisburg: Morehouse, 2010), 13.

to be the crowning glory of creation, but to partner with God in tending the earth and bringing the plans for the garden to their fulfilment. It's through Adam that the shrubs appear and the plants spring up and, later, it's through Adam that the animals get their names.[3] These creative assignments are offered to Adam and others are offered to us. We can say no just as Adam could have said no to working the land or naming the animals but there are things that only we can create and will remain latent if we don't create them. When we say yes to engaging our creativity, we—and our world— become more fully who we were made to be.

This yes to engaging our sacred creativity doesn't mean committing to work earnestly to make perfect things that somehow earn us favour or status with God. While beautiful things reveal God in their own way, it's less the product of our creativity that matters and more the quality of the creative expression that comes through it. The sign that we're joining God as co-creators is when our creative energy echoes God's own. As Genesis makes clear, God doesn't create under pressure or due to necessity. God's creativity is spontaneous and joyful and gloriously unhurried. God rests not only at the end of the creative venture, but in between each of the days. Freedom and playfulness characterise God's creativity far more than discipline and rigidity.

Watching my children has helped me better to understand creativity, both human and divine. From forts and Lego creations to paintings and stories, they approach creativity with joy and spontaneity and in the spirit of play. They are unafraid to waste time and get caught up in the flow of their activity. They create for the joy of creating more than to achieve any kind of success; and, so, they continue to make whether anyone is watching or not. The product is secondary to the process of making, and an unfinished creation is not failure but a sign that the creative project has evolved. They have

---

[3] Gen 2.5; Gen 2.19-20.

shown me the essential roles of imagination, of flexible thought and faith in the possibility of something new. They have also taught me that attention is central to creativity—both because it's through attending to their world and themselves that they get their ideas and because when they are making they are completely absorbed. My children are amateurs and proudly so. They love (*amare*) what they do and it's that love that makes their creating worthwhile. I hope they will always know unselfconscious freedom and joy in their creativity. I hope that they might prompt you to remember and return to your own childhood creativity.

Also helpful along the journey into embracing sacred creativity has been finding a home in expressive art. This came as a revelation. I had assumed that expressive art was a sort of meta practice, only available to the masters such as Matisse and Picasso who had learnt the rules, perfected their technique and had all the tools available to them. Only these artists were free to focus on simply expressing themselves in colour and line. More recently, with the help of contemplative artists such as Christine Valters Paintner, I've accepted that expressive art is not just for the technically advanced but is, instead, a way of creating art that is less about results and more about process. It's a way of creating that helps me to tap back into my childhood way of creating, that I see so clearly revealed in my own children. This art can be as simple as a doodle or a wash of colour or a collage of found objects or images, but it connects us to what is around and within us in an immediate, intuitive way, and can help us to bring to light hidden wounds, longings, and insights.

But how exactly does creativity become prayer? When is drawing a picture or making music or baking a cake just drawing a picture or making music or baking a cake and when does it become prayer?

First of all, it's important to say what does not make it become prayer. It's not only when the picture or music (or cake!) we're creating has some overtly religious connotation. Abstract pictures, photographs of trees, and jazz music can be just as prayerful as paintings of Jesus, photographs of churches, and worship music. And yet, it's not the case that everything human beings make is created prayerfully. Things that are created to harm or hurt cannot be created prayerfully because to intentionally harm is against the movement of God's love in our world. Indeed, I wonder if these destructive things can be considered creations at all. Because I believe that our creative acts participate in God's own life-bringing creativity, I struggle to acknowledge that using creativity for a destructive end is properly creative.

What does make our creativity prayerful is our intention as we create. When we create prayerfully we engage our creativity with the intention to be co-creators; to be caught up in the flow of divine creativity that enfolds, inspires and guides us as innately creative beings.

> What makes our creativity prayerful is our intention as we create.

Sometimes that means seeking to make some specific thing that will bring greater life, joy, understanding or healing, either for ourselves or for others, such as when we create a meal to be enjoyed by guests or when we compose a poem to give voice to whatever is unfolding within. Sometimes it means letting go of an end altogether and allowing ourselves to enjoy becoming present to the process of joining self with medium and art form as when we lose ourselves in painting or singing. At these times, we're usually so lost in our creativity that we don't stop to reflect on it as prayer. It's not until afterwards that we become aware of its mysteriously prayerful quality.

Both of these ways of creating realise our capacity to be the presence through which God continues to create us and our world, renewing us as we make things new. We open ourselves to the divine creative energy already around and within us and become one with its flow through us. We more fully receive our creativity as a gift to be offered and ourselves as witnesses invited to participate.

For those of us with a particularly vocal or aggressive inner critic, it can be difficult to claim our own creative identity. Even if we want to express our creative soul, we may be blocked by fear or anticipated shame that we'll be unable to create what we intend and that we'll be diminished through the process of trying. If you can relate to this you may find it helpful to nurture a more "useless" approach to creativity, actively seeking ways you can create with no goal or purpose (for example, by enjoying watching paint mix with water or through stream of consciousness writing). You might also find it helpful to make your inner critic the object rather than the judge of the creative process, perhaps by dialogue journaling with it or by personifying it through painting or with words.

For those still struggling to accept or express their creativity, a smaller, more manageable step into praying with creativity might be to draw on the fruits of the creativity of others. We can, for example, read poetry prayerfully, joining our voices with those we read and allowing imagery and verse to open us to God in new ways. We can also pray with images and colour, seeking God in and through what we see. One such practice is *visio divina*, in which we read images with our eyes and allow them to guide us deeper. These ways of praying with the creativity of others are no less valuable or worthwhile than praying in and through our own making. They may even offer a gentle pathway into praying with our own creativity by inspiring us to join our own voices, imagery, and thoughts with those of others as we seek to respond to God.

This section contains a variety of creative prayer practices to get you started in using your creativity to pray. There are practices centred on photography, poetry, music and dance. There are several ways to pray with visual art, both through making it and by looking at it. Also included is a laughter prayer. While laughter can be a tool of the critic, used to embarrass, dismiss and mock, it can also become a pathway to self-forgetful joy when it grounds, connects, and relaxes us. This friendly laughter gently disarms the inner critic and keeps our creativity God-oriented rather than success-driven.

As such, a willingness to be surprised and amused by ourselves, the world and our work can greatly aid us in our creativity.

Even if you don't tend to see yourself as an artist, dancer, or photographer, I encourage you to play with these practices; hold them loosely as you approach them with curiosity. It's important, however, that you don't see these suggestions as in any way limiting the forms that creative prayer can take. Beneath the individual practices of this chapter is the deeper invitation to turn any of the ways in which humans express their creativity into prayer, simply by recognising that God is the source, end and flow of all creativity. This flings wide the doors to turning every meal we cook, every room we decorate, every outfit we put together, every letter we write, and every rhythm we establish into a prayerful act. All of these ways of creating can become an opening onto deeper relationship with God and innermost self if we begin with this as our intention.

For reflection

What did you enjoy creating when you were a child?

In what ways does your creativity find expression today?

What blocks you from expressing your creativity?

PHOTOGRAPHY AND PRAYER

Most of us have a camera or a smartphone and we tend to snap photographs without much more than a passing thought. This practice will slow you down and encourage a more prayerful approach to how you use your camera and view your photographs.

Practising

~ Decide where you would like to pray with your camera. You may like to go somewhere you often find yourself taking photos, a favourite place or room perhaps. Or you may prefer to explore somewhere new and undocumented. Perhaps you would like to pray with your camera throughout a day. A helpful way to begin is simply by taking your camera with you on a familiar walk.

~ Agree with yourself how many photographs you will take. This will help to sharpen your attention. You may like to resolve to take just one or two photos.

~ Allow yourself some time to settle and prepare yourself. Close your eyes. Notice the darkness and imagine the beginning of creation, before light and colour burst forth. Deepen and slow your breath. In this quiet place, ask God: "What do you want me to notice today?"

~ Let this question guide you as you pick up your camera or phone. Go slowly and try to allow your intuition to lead rather than overthinking the process.

~ Later, take some time to reflectively view the photo or photos. You may like to experiment with setting your filter to black-and-white.

~ Reflecting on one photo, ask yourself these questions:

What do you notice?

What feature or shadow or colour stands out to you?

What does the black and white version reveal that the colour one did not?

What does your choice of angle or perspective say about you and/or your subject?

What does the image stir in you?

How does this image invite prayer?

~ Consider journaling your thoughts or conversation with God or print out the photo as a reminder of this prayerful time.

DOODLE PRAYERS

You don't need to be a great artist to pray through art-making. This practice is based on an exercise in *Praying in Color* by Sybil Macbeth and requires nothing more than a piece of paper, a pen, and a willingness to experiment.

Practising

~ Start with a blank piece of paper.

~ In the centre, write a word or phrase of significance. It could be a name for God, the name of someone for whom you're praying, a Scripture verse, a line from a poem or a question you have.

~ Draw a shape around the words to start the doodle. This is your prayer space. Start to doodle around it, releasing your words to God in prayer. Doodle in silence or talk to God, if you feel led.

~ Add other people, other names for God, or other verses or questions to your paper. Draw a shape around each set of new words to create a separate prayer space. Doodle around these and pray.

~ Pause and say "amen" between each prayer space you add.

~ Once you feel your doodle prayer is finished, take some time to sit with what you have created. Notice where your attention is drawn and if there are any patterns or conflicts, but don't force insight or understanding. Allow your presence to your doodles and words to become part of your prayer.

COLOUR MEDITATION

Expressive art can be a wonderful opening onto prayer. In expressive art, we join ourselves with our materials and express what is stirring within as a way of becoming more present, more aware, and more open to the Spirit. This meditation focuses on colour and requires only a coloured pencil and a piece of paper.

Practising

~ Choose a coloured pencil. Don't overthink your choice. Pick the one you feel drawn to in this moment.

~ Befriend your pencil. Look at it. What do you notice? Try to name its shade. What does it remind you of? Feel it. Move your fingers over its various surfaces. Smell it. Does it have a scent?

~ Begin to explore colour using your pencil. Be playful. Experiment with different pressure and speed and strokes. Listen to what your pencil asks to show you. Be attentive to the space between your pencil and paper—a holy space, pregnant with possibility. There is no right approach or result. You don't need to share what you produce with anyone else. It is between you, your materials and God.

~ After a couple of minutes, ask yourself: What is emerging? What is asking to be revealed or extended? How else might you explore your pencil?

~ After five minutes, look at what is emerging with compassion. If you notice judgement arising, remember that your creativity is a sharing in God's own creativity. It is a gift and is precious. Honour your work as a token of your divinely given creativity.

~ As you look with compassion on your work, what do you notice? What do you notice on the page? What do you notice within yourself? What are you drawn to? Does anything seem out of place? How does what you see resonate with you and your life? Are any memories arising? Does it stir any desires or fears?

~ After ten minutes, look again. Let yourself sink into the colour. Close your eyes and allow yourself to soak in it. Know that this colour is an expression of light. See if you can accept that you, too, are an expression of light—with a unique shade—and that you are held in the great Artist's hand as your life emerges on the paper of creation.

~ Close with a few minutes of silence. Let yourself rest in God's love. Whatever is tight...allow it to loosen. Whatever you have worked to hide...allow it to be seen. Bring your whole self into the safe presence of God.

An icon is a particular sort of image, a sacred piece of art rooted in a rich tradition of prayer. To the modern eye they may appear primitive or childlike because they do not follow the traditional rules of perspective. This is not a mistake. In icons, the perspective is reversed so that the one looking at the icon is the one who is seen. The icon is not the object of our gaze but draws our gaze into and beyond itself to the reality of what is depicted—namely, the saint and the presence of God. Icons fill Orthodox churches and most Orthodox households have at least one icon.

Icons have been controversial throughout the Church's history, notably during the 8th and 9th centuries when a vicious dispute arose about whether icons broke the second commandment. Eventually, a distinction was made between worship (which is only appropriately offered to God) and veneration (which is an honour that can appropriately be offered to icons for their capacity to guide prayer and open hearts to God).

Increasingly, people from all denominations of the church are coming to see the value in praying with icons. In our highly visual age, icons challenge some of the less healthy ways of seeing that are commonplace in our societies. The gaze that we use when we pray with icons is soft, open, and receptive with the ability to guide us through the visible to the invisible. And, as Henri Nouwen explains in *Behold the Beauty of the Lord*, icons not only help to focus our gaze and attention on God in the midst of a world full of distraction, but they also serve as schools of active seeing, reshaping the way we see and relate to other people and creatures. The icon reminds us that each person, no matter how imperfect, is a bearer of God's image and encourages us to respond to them as such.

If you'd like to try praying with icons, replicas are available in religious bookstores and online and an internet search will quickly bring up many images. If, though, you find yourself particularly intrigued by or enjoy praying with images or replicas of icons, I encourage you to try to find a real one as the prayerful process through which they are written (the term for the creation of an icon) saturates their physical form and is part of how they guide prayer. Many cathedrals and churches now have icons, so you don't need to find an Orthodox church—although, of course, you will find many there.

Practising

~ Decide which icon you will use and how long you will spend in contemplation (20 minutes is suggested). Find a comfortable place where you can gaze at your chosen icon. Traditionally, pray-ers stand before icons.

~ Express your intention to encounter God and ask God to guide you during your prayer time.

~ Try to let your attention descend from head to heart, allowing yourself to become present to this moment. It may help to place your hand on your heart.

~ Let your heart-based attention soften your gaze and look at the icon. Receive it as a mystical window with you on one side and the reality that is depicted on the other. The gold represents the presence of God breaking through.

~ Let the icon "speak" to you by allowing it to draw your gaze. Let yourself be led, maintaining heart-centred attention. You don't need to analyse what is happening, try to stay open to the unfolding.

~ End the contemplation with a prayer of gratitude.

~ Afterwards, you might like to spend some time in quiet reflection asking yourself what it was like to look at the icon with the eyes of your heart and remembering what drew your gaze. Also, give yourself space to become aware of any resistance and wonder about where it came from and why. Notice how you feel after the experience and if you feel drawn to try again another time.

VISIO DIVINA

Visio divina translates as "divine seeing" and is a method of praying with images that builds on the principles of *lectio divina*. Instead of Scripture or text, this form of prayer focuses our attention on visual elements. *Visio divina* also borrows from the rich tradition of praying with icons but expands the range of images that can be used as prayerful guides.

Practising
~ Pick out a favourite image, painting or photograph.

~ Breathe and prepare your eyes to receive the image before you. Ask for the gift of vision: to see beneath the surface of things.

~ Open your eyes and gaze with the eyes of your heart. This is a gentle and receptive looking, not a harsh stare.

~ Move your eyes over the image with both reverence and curiosity. Take your time. Notice colours, textures, lines, light, shadow and flow.

~ Notice if there is a particular area that attracts your attention. Allow your eyes to rest there.

~ Open your imagination to any connections that might be stirring: memories, dreams, feelings.

~ Listen for how you are being invited in this moment. Open yourself to receive whatever may come. Hold it lightly, resisting the urge to analyse or judge. Simply receive.

~ Gently release the image you have been looking at by closing your eyes and returning to your breath. Sink into stillness.

~ Offer gratitude for the ways in which this image has touched your heart.

~ Afterwards, it may be helpful to journal or express artistically what you experienced in praying with the image. Don't worry if you can't make complete sense of what arose during this time. Instead, record the experience without judgement and continue to pray for insight and understanding.

LAUGHING WITH GOD

Humour is essential to creativity as it keeps us playful, open, and spontaneous. Without gentle, light-hearted humour, we can easily become perfectionistic, self-critical, and stuck. In *Praying with Body and Soul*, Jane Vennard suggests that paying attention to what makes us laugh and sharing that with God can help to guide us into a more joyful, open-hearted prayer life. She notes the connection between laughing and loving and quotes Rick Bernardo who, in his article 'A Serious Meditation on Laughter' writes that "it's difficult not to love someone when you are laughing with them."[4] This practice encourages you to notice what amuses you and suggests a pathway for sharing that with God. This can then be incorporated into your creative prayer practices as a way of diffusing tension and keeping your focus on enjoying God's loving presence with you in the process.

Practising

~ Throughout your day, actively seek out the moments that amuse you, delight you or make you laugh. Vennard suggests thinking of this task as a treasure hunt for the humorous in life and recommends carrying a small notebook in which these moments can be jotted down.

~ Each time you discover a humorous moment, take a moment to offer your amusement to God. This can be through a smile or laugh, with words or some other spontaneous expression of delight. You may like to imagine God, perhaps in the form of Jesus, laughing with you. If you are writing these moments down, consider taking some time at the end of each day or week, to review all that has amused you and to share your delight with God.

---

[4] Jane Vennard, *Praying with Body and Soul: A Way to Intimacy with God* (Minneapolis: Augsburg, 1998), 66.

A note for those who have been hurt by laughter

Vennard acknowledges that some of us have been hurt
by laughter in the past. It's important to note that the
laughter that is aligned with love is friendly and
companionable, not dismissive or cruel. God is not
amused by laughter that wounds and will not laugh at
those who are hurting. If, as you try out this practice,
you find yourself remembering being wounded by
laughter or feeling diminished by humour, share those
feelings with God and ask for the comfort, protection,
and healing you need. You may also like to see if you
can become open to remembering when laughter has
felt refreshing or joyful and notice what physical or
emotional sensations are present. These can guide you
in recognising when laughter is offered as a balm and
blessing rather than a punishment or belittling.

HAND DANCE PRAYER

Dancing can be a powerful way of connecting with God through
embodied movement rather than words and is available to all, no
matter their degree of talent or expertise. In her book *The Artist's
Rule*, Christine Valters Paintner suggests that limiting movement to
the hands, can be a helpful entryway to exploring dance as prayer. If
you find yourself intrigued by dance as prayer but are not sure how
to start, this practice is a good place to begin. As you find yourself
becoming more comfortable with engaging your hands in prayerful
expression, you can introduce more of your body in the movement.

Practising

~ Begin by selecting a song or piece of music that draws you to prayer with which you deeply resonate or which reminds you of the presence of God.

~ With one hand in front, explore the space around you. Move your hand through the air in front of you. Play with different speeds and shapes. Explore how far you can reach and then rest your hand somewhere on your body and feel the physical connection. Then, rest your hand somewhere else and pause.

~ Play the song you have selected. Again, move your hand but allow the music to guide your hand. Trust this process and try not to think it through. Maintain a curiosity about what you see unfolding. Notice how your hand wants to explore the space around you and allow it to lead. Continue to move just one hand or allow both to become involved. As you move, offer your thoughts and feelings, your desires and fears to God.

~ When the song ends, rest for a moment and experience the music and movement vibrating through you. Pay attention to your inner stirrings. Is there a shape or simple motion that feels like a fitting conclusion to this experience? Create a gesture or movement that represents this and rest in that expression.

AUDIO DIVINA

Music and prayer are intertwined in almost all spiritual traditions, across both time and geography. Throughout the Judeo-Christian tradition, music has a privileged place in worship and devotion, not simply as embellishment but as prayerful expression.

The Bible's prayer book, the Psalms, is also the Bible's songbook and many scholars believe that some of the more poetic passages in Paul's letters were the hymns of the early Church.[5] This entwining of prayer and music has echoed through the ages, with influential writers such as Augustine, Aquinas and Hildegard of Bingen affirming music's ability to unlock and express the soul's love for God, as well as to connect praying people and creation in a shared expression of praise and longing. While the 16th century reformation of the western Church saw many spiritual practices stripped away, music was the last to be taken, with the pivotal reformer Martin Luther affirming the traditional view that music is an "excellent gift of God," found throughout creation and rightly offered by human beings as a central part of their prayer and worship.[6]

There are many ways to pray with music and, as always, there is freedom to explore and experiment with different methods. Here I offer a holy listening (*audio divina*) practice, followed by a couple of ways it can be modified, developed and extended. This practice builds on versions of audio divina offered by Christine Valters Paintner and Teresa Blythe[7] as well as my own experience of praying with music. It can be explored using a range of musical forms, including your own voice and the music of nature, already and always surrounding you.

---

[5] For example, Romans 11:33-36, Philippians 2:6-11, Colossians 1:15-20, 1 Timothy 3:16, and Heb 1:3-4.

[6] "First then, looking at music itself, you will find that from the beginning of the world it has been instilled and implanted in all creatures, individually and collectively. For nothing is without sound or harmony. Even the air, which of itself is invisible and imperceptible to all our senses, and which, since it lacks both voice and speech, is the least musical of all things, becomes sonorous, audible, and comprehensible when it is set in motion...Music is still more wonderful in living things, especially birds...And yet, compared to the human voice, all this hardly deserves the name of music, so abundant and incomprehensible is here the munificence and wisdom of our most gracious Creator...next to the Word of God, music deserves the highest praise." Martin Luther, "Preface to Georg Rhau's Symphoniae iucundae," in *Luther's Works*, vol. 53 (Minneapolis: Fortress Press, 1965), 321-322.

[7] See Christine Valters Paintner, *Lectio Divina, the Sacred Art: Transforming Words and Images into Heart-Centered Prayer* (Woodstock, VT: Skylight Paths Publishing, 2011), and Teresa Blythe, *50 Ways to Pray: Practices from Many Traditions and Times* (Nashville: Abingdon Press, 2006).

Practising

~ Decide which musical form you would like to pray with. You can choose any piece of music you like: it could be a song or hymn or it could be instrumental. Christine Valters Paintner recommends beginning with instrumental music "for the sake of simplicity" and notes that lyrics "add another layer of complexity to pay attention to." Her suggestion is Bach's "Sarabande" movements from his Solo Suites for Cello. Teresa Blythe recommends beginning with a piece from a genre "that inspires you" or which has "moved you in some way previously." I also recommend the music of the Taizé community which centres on simple musical forms and short repeated lines that encourage meditation rather than analysis.

~ Before you press play, take a moment to settle. Deepen your breathing and notice the rise and fall of your abdomen as you create space to receive air. Paintner suggests imagining a "wide open space being hollowed out within you as a sacred space in which to listen to the music."

~ As you breathe in, see if you can affirm your intention to allow music to be your guide, both into the present moment and into prayerful expression and response. As you breathe out, see if you can gently acknowledge and release anything that might be standing in the way or you being present to this prayerful experience.

~ Play the music for the first time, letting it wash over you as you feel the vibrations in your body.

~ Listen with openness and curiosity. If you have chosen a piece you are familiar with, try to listen to it as though for the first time. Notice its rhythm, melody, tone, and dynamics as well as the lyrics, if there are any. Allow this noticing to include your body as well as mind. If your breathing or body wants to move with the music, let it. Don't analyse your movement; let the music guide you into a deeper form of listening and intuitive self-expression.

~ Listen again. Notice what stands out or shimmers, either in the music or in you. What is being offered to you? Again, try to allow this noticing to include your whole self. It may come through tears or emotion rather than with a word or image. See if you can accept whatever comes, receiving it like a gift you can open in your own time.

~ When the music ends, allow it to continue to echo inside you. What do you notice stirring within?

~ Sit with whatever has come up during this time, trusting in God's presence with you. Allow yourself to be led deeper and be attentive to any invitation to respond.

~ End by acknowledging and then gently releasing your thoughts, feelings, noticings, bodily sensations. Do this in whatever way feels right, perhaps with a bodily posture rather than words. Allow yourself to become still, simply enjoying being with God and allowing what has happened to sink deeper.

Instead of practicing *audio divina* solely by listening, you could sing or play an instrument along with the music. If you know the music well, you can sing or play the tune or harmony but, even if you don't, you can still join in the music-making through improvisation. You don't have to be a talented musician to do this. The aim is not to create a perfect musical form but to help to connect you with the music as a way of listening to (and receiving from) it deeply. One suggestion is to hum and hold a note from the music and notice the harmony it creates as well as the vibration in your throat and chest.

You could also listen with a pen and paper, or other artistic media, in hand. Let the music guide your hand in a free expression of what you hear in the music or notice within you. You may find yourself drawn to following the dynamics or the rhythm rather than the melody or words. Afterwards, spend some time with your art, looking at it with curiosity, not judgement. Ask yourself what you notice and allow that to guide you in prayer, freely sharing whatever comes with God.

PANTOUM POETRY AS PRAYER

When we try to express our deepest feelings and thoughts with words it is often images or solitary words or phrases that come, rather than coherent prose. A *pantoum* poem offers a pathway to praying with just what comes, without the pressure of stitching them into flowing prose. This is a simple verse form that uses repeating lines to create flow and rhythm and I was first introduced to it as a prayerful practice by Christine Valters Paintner.[8] Here, I have suggested that you begin your *pantoum* by identifying something that speaks to you about God's love or presence, but you could use any experience, feeling or thought as a starting point.

Practising

~ Begin by acknowledging your desire to go beneath the surface of yourself and your experience, and your openness to God with you in this process.

~ Ask yourself: what or who speaks to you of God's love or presence? You may like to limit yourself to reflecting on today or this week. As you reflect on the person, place, thing, feeling or concept, notice what colours, images, shapes, memories and feelings are stirred in you.

~ Without judging what comes, write down your thoughts. You can make notes or write in continuous prose. Use sensual and descriptive language as much as possible. Allow yourself to be surprised by what emerges in the process.

~ Re-read your reflection and underline at least six images or phrases that stand out, that seem surprising or evoke a response within you. You can edit lightly at this point, but keep your focus on clarifying rather than correcting.

~ Take your underlined phrases and enter them into the *pantoum* form that follows. Don't overthink this. Once you have filled in the six phrases, go back and follow the instructions for the remaining lines on the form and fill them in as directed.

---

[8] See Christine Valters Paintner, *The Artist's Rule: Nurturing your Creative Soul with Monastic Wisdom* (Notre Dame: Sorin Books, 2011).

~ Take a few minutes to read the poem that has emerged. What feelings arise as you read it? Feel free to edit for clarity or flow but don't change so much that you lose the rawness of your experience of the presence of God.

~ Read the poem out loud as a prayer of thanksgiving for God's presence in your life. Listen for how God is inviting you deeper into that awareness.

Structure of a French *Pantoum*

Stanza 1
Line1:
Line 2:
Line 3:
Line 4:

Stanza 2
Line 5: *repeat of line 2 in stanza 1*
Line 6: *new line*
Line 7: *repeat of line 4 in stanza 1*
Line 8: *new line*

Stanza 3
Line 9: *repeat line 6 of stanza 2*
Line 10: *repeat line 3 of stanza 1*
Line 11: *repeat line 8 of stanza 2*
Line 12: *repeat line 1 of stanza 1*

Praying with Technology

It's a sign of my age that I remember a time before the internet and mobile phones. One of my earliest memories is of sitting, aged 3, on the little wooden chair in our hallway, fiddling with the spiral phone cord while my mum dialled the number of a friend. I'd come home from playgroup with a chunk of hair missing and my mum wanted to establish the truth of my claim that 'Amie did it.' A few rings of the phone and a couple of minutes of conversation later, Mum hung up. It turned out that Amie also had a chunk of hair missing; we'd been playing hairdressers.

As I let my mind wander through the hallways of memory, I notice how many others are connected with now-extinct forms of technology. I remember, for example, my delight when my parents bought a roaming handset for the house phone. No longer did I run the risk of my sisters overhearing my conversations in the hall but could grab the handset and run to the privacy of my bedroom. Of course, there was always the chance they would pick up another handset in a different room and listen in but usually I'd hear them breathing and yell at them to "get off the phone!" It wasn't until I got my first, brick sized, mobile phone aged 17 that I could finally make calls without the risk of them listening in but those were the days of 30-minute phone plans with 50 free texts, so we had to choose our words carefully.

I remember doing all my homework without any use of copy and paste or Wikipedia. If I needed to research something, I had no choice but to read a book or consult a wise adult, and if I wanted to check the definition of a word, I had to open the heavy dictionary we kept downstairs. There was no Google, and even when there was, I spent a couple of years avoiding it, feeling overwhelmed by the number of results that would load in response to a simple question. More than once, I remember thinking that the internet was a fad that wouldn't last.

I also remember a time when "friend" meant someone you actually know well, like and trust rather than someone you met once and then added on Facebook so they could view your life in pictures and captions. In those days, no one claimed to have a thousand friends and photos were images developed at a chemist while you waited with bated breath to see if you'd managed not to cut off peoples' heads and legs.

I review these memories with a mixture of nostalgia and amazement. Nostalgia because, barring some sort of global disaster, we'll never return to an age without technology; amazement because I realise how dependent I've become on things that I once lacked entirely. I marvel at how I managed with 30 minutes and 50 texts when nowadays I spend hours on phone or Zoom calls and send hundreds of messages each week. I wonder how I found the answer to all the obscure questions I now ask the internet. I notice how hard I would find it to be limited with the number of photos I take of my children and how disappointing it would be to find out all the photos from a birthday party or family vacation had been ruined by having my finger over the lens.

I'm told that the fact that I remember a time pre-internet and yet am now dependent on it makes me an Xennial—someone born between the years 1975 and 1985. We're a small group, caught between the older Generation X and the younger Millennials, who had an analogue childhood and a digital adulthood. It would be nice to think that because we grew up without mobiles, internet or iPads we're less likely to be addicted to technology than younger people but, at least in my case, this is simply not true. Time and again I've had to confront the extent of my dependency on technology and, in particular, my tendency to spend too many hours on my phone, replying to emails and texts, browsing the internet or scrolling through social media.

A few years ago, recognising this dependency on my phone, I decided to give up social media for Lent. Not only was it absorbing an excessive amount of my time, but it was also increasing my anxiety. I struggled to be present, my mind racing through scenarios and jumping from thought to thought. I was also in the midst of a period of dryness in prayer. I found it hard to still and centre myself, I couldn't find the "right" time and, whenever I did enter into prayer, I was distracted. I hoped that by fasting from social media I would create more time and space to be intentional about my time with God, to access my quiet centre and find the connection, rest and direction I was misguidedly looking for in a newsfeed.

I deleted the apps from my phone and immediately felt liberated. I knew I'd developed unhealthy patterns of behaviour and it was a relief to know I'd put on the brakes.

After a while, though, it became more of a struggle. I noticed my tendency to reach for my phone during moments of boredom or anxiety in an attempt to distract or numb myself. Sometimes I was seized by FOMO (fear of missing out) and was tempted to abandon my fast to check I wasn't being left out of anything important. More than once I gave in to that temptation.

Slowly though, I learnt that better than caving in was to take some deep breaths and use my senses to anchor myself back in the present. When I noticed that urge to check or scroll, I'd ask myself what I could see or hear or touch or smell and this would help me to detach, just a little, from my feelings of boredom or anxiety. This became a new way of praying because each time I released my desire for distraction or fantasy, I affirmed my desire to be present with God in the here and now. Those deep breaths were tiny acts of surrender and intentionally engaging with my senses became a way of listening to God's invitation to return to the reality of my life and God's presence in it. Often my sensory re-grounding practice would open onto a few minutes of silence in

> When we release our desire for distraction or fantasy, we affirm our desire to be present with God in the here and now.

which I would sit with God in whatever was happening within, gently releasing thoughts, images and anxiety with my breath.

By Easter, I was the same me—just more at peace and with less mental junk blocking me from being present. I had learnt to notice and hold open the clear spaces in my day, and because of that it'd become easier to pray. It wasn't so much that the empty spaces gave me time to pray but that my noticing of these clear spaces had become prayer. In those moments, instead of feeling bored or anxious, I would sense a kind of already-here fullness and would linger in order to better soak it in.

I wasn't in a rush to add social media apps back to my phone but after a while I realised I was missing birthdays and announcements. I reinstalled the apps (a moment of weakness, perhaps) but this time activated a timer to limit how long I spent on the apps each day. Now, a few years later, I think I may need to take another break. I confess to fiddling with the timers to give myself "just a bit longer" and I also notice myself falling back into a pattern of boredom scrolling.

Technology, and social media in particular, is designed to be addictive and it's healthy to take a regular break, whether that comes in the form of a Lenten fast, a weekly day or evening off, or a daily pause. But while we can find ways to resist it encroaching into every part of our lives, it's difficult to separate ourselves from it altogether. Technology is a fact of our modern Western lives and in many ways it's a blessing. It's because of technology that I can remain connected with family and friends even when we're miles apart. It's technology that allows me to speak to those in hospital even when I'm unable to visit in person. And very often it's via technology that I gain an insight into the lives and work of those in very different places and situations to me and which feeds my compassion and motivates my activity in the world. Perhaps you can add more examples.

All of this makes me wonder if there is another way to look at the relationship between technology and prayer. I tend to see technology as the enemy of prayer, endlessly snatching me away from quiet moments with God, but what if I suspended my suspicion and looked for the places of intersection, the ways in which technology might feed or nourish my prayer?

This isn't the first time in Christian history that changes in the cultural milieu have prompted a change in the way people worship and pray. Before the conversion of Constantine in 312 it was illegal to be Christian which meant most Christians gathered secretly in homes or house churches. It was only after his conversion that buildings specifically designed to be churches began to be built and a regular, formalised pattern of public prayer and worship was established. Similarly, before the invention of the printing press most people didn't have their own copy of the Bible. It was in the wake of this invention and the accompanying Reformation that Bibles were translated into vernacular languages and widely dispersed for the use of the laity in their personal devotions.

> What if we suspend our suspicion and look for places of intersection, the ways in which technology might feed or nourish prayer?

Opinions vary as to whether these developments helped or hindered the Church in its call to be a life-giving and fruit-bearing presence in the world. Arguably Constantine's conversion forced the Church to become a worldly institution and forced it to develop in a more imperial and less Christlike direction and some believe that the advent of the printing press and the sudden availability of written materials for private consumption paved the way to a more individualistic faith, less rooted in community.[1]

---

[1] Some thinkers, including Canadian philosopher Charles Taylor, Scottish sociologist Steve Bruce and American historian Brad Gregory also see the Reformation as a major cause of the secularisation of the West. See Charles Taylor, *A Secular Age* (Cambridge, Mass: Belknap Press, 2007), Steve Bruce,

And yet there were also opportunities and possibilities that came with and through these cultural shifts. Constantine's conversion put an end to the persecution of Christians in the Roman Empire and opened up all sorts of creative opportunities for communal worship and spiritual expression, while the printing press made the Bible accessible to ordinary people and challenged the excessive power and frequent abuses of the institutional church. While neither came without a shadow, there was gift in both.

Similarly, there will be disagreement about the moral or spiritual value of the changes that have come through the rapid expansion of technology and it's rare to find someone who is entirely positive about its implications. I know from conversation with others that I'm not alone in my wrestling with technology and its tendency to take me away from the embodied present. And yet, as with Constantine's conversion and the creation of the printing press, the changes to our milieu made through technological advances also provide opportunities and possibilities for our spiritual lives. Perhaps, then, the task before us is not to decide whether to label technology good or bad for prayer or spiritual living but to seek to notice how, when and where it nourishes prayer and how, when and where it tends to starve it.

How this looks in practice may differ between individuals and groups and may change over time. What nourishes one person may starve another. There will be times when the possibilities opened to us through technology (through apps, virtual networks, and podcasts, for example) invite our exploration and there will be times when we have good reasons to resist them. One approach will not fit all and an openness to play and be curious is essential as well as a willingness to reflect and change course if it becomes apparent that something has become problematic and is distracting or numbing us from lovingly looking at the real.

I can offer you no simple formula for discerning this, but I've found that maintaining a detached curiosity is helpful. This curiosity

Secularization (Oxford: OUP, 2011), and Brad Gregory, *The Unintended Reformation* (Cambridge, MA: Belknap, 2012).

is open and spacious without being naive or dismissive. The new is neither rejected out of hand nor pursued blindly. Underlying is a recognition that what is given is always already enough and yet God delights in surprising us.

I've also found that seeking harmony can be helpful in stabilising my spiritual life. Instead of jumping from the tried-and-tested to the new-and-exciting and back again in a futile quest for a spiritual hit, I'm learning to look for the places of possibility where the old and new are not in conflict but seem to add texture or depth to one another. I've found it helpful to ask myself: where can technology help to bring what I already know to be life-giving into better rhythm with my relationships, my routines, my responsibilities and all the other givens of my life?

The following practices are rooted in an awareness of both the capacity of technology to open onto prayer and its tendency to distract from or replace the real. Some of the practices suggest ways in which you might use technology in your prayer life, while others offer pathways to a more reflective and intentional use of technology. I've also included an invitation to fast from a form of technology you find particularly addictive. My hope is that you might explore all these ways of engaging with – and disengaging from – technology but, as always, try to trust where and how God's Spirit is prompting you.

For reflection

In what ways has technology been a blessing in your life? How has it been problematic?

When do you notice yourself becoming disturbed or unsettled by technology?

When or how do you fast from technology?

PRAYING THE HOURS
WITH PHONE ALARMS

Praying the hours is an ancient practice built upon these words from Psalm 119: "seven times a day I praise you."[2] The practice of praying at fixed hours several times a day originated in Judaism and was quickly adopted and developed by the early church (Acts 10:3, 10:9 and 16:25 all suggest that the communities prayed at various times in the day). The second and third century writings of Church Fathers such as Clement of Alexandria, Origen and Tertullian refer to the practice of morning and evening prayer and of the prayers at terce (third hour), sext (sixth hour) and none (ninth hour). In the sixth century, St Benedict formalised the practice by naming each hour. Praying the hours has since formed the basis of prayer for many monks and nuns, although today the times of individual prayers vary. For more on the history of praying the hours as well as suggestions for prayer for these times I recommend *The Little Book of Hours: Praying with the Community of Jesus* by The Community of Jesus and *Praying the Hours in Ordinary Life* by Lauralee Farrer.

The long history of this way of praying may make it intimidating to a beginner. If you recognise yourself as a beginner, it's important to remember that underlying the practice is the rhythm of regular prayer throughout the day. While the fixed times and assigned prayers for each of the hours offer the traditional pathway into establishing this rhythm and building community amongst the praying Church across the ages, any way in which we build a rhythm of prayer into our day builds on the tradition of praying the hours and connects us with the broader church family.

It can, however, be difficult to remember to pray at these times, especially in our overstuffed lives. In ancient times, the early Church community in Rome used the secular Roman forum bells to remind them to pray, and churches and monasteries often use their own bells to call the community to prayer. In the absence of such bells,

---

[2] Psalm 119:164.

we can continue this tradition by using our phone alarms to remind us to pause and pray.

Practising

~ Set an alarm on your phone to go off several times throughout the day. Below are the traditional hours. If you don't want to be awakened in the night you can combine vigils with compline, and lauds with prime. You can also experiment with praying at different times than the ones listed below. The idea is to build a prayerful rhythm of returning to interior awareness of God's presence throughout the day rather than to follow rigidly a prescribed pattern of outward behaviour.

~ When your alarm goes off, pray however you feel led. You may like to use a prayer from the daily office, or to offer a breath prayer (a few words in rhythm with inhale and exhale). Alternatively, you may simply want to pause and sit in silence for a minute of two, allowing your day to be punctuated with rest.

The Canonical Hours

Vigils: *during the night, at about 2 a.m.*

Lauds: *at dawn, the time varies by season*

Prime: *first hour, approximately 6 a.m.*

Terce: *third hour, approximately 9 a.m.*

Sext: *sixth hour, approximately 12 noon*

None: *ninth hour, approximately 3 p.m.*

Vespers: *at "the lighting of the lamps," about 6 p.m.*

Compline: *before retiring, about 9p.m.*

A simple way to use technology to enhance your prayer life is to draw on the many guided prayer practices that are available online. Some of these are available via podcasts, some via email subscription, and some via websites. Below are some of my favourites:

Pray As You Go: This podcast is offered by the British Society of Jesuits and guides the listener through a meditation on a passage from Scripture prescribed for the day by the Catholic church. It features music, readings and questions, and includes time to reflect and pray as you listen.

Prayer from the Taizé Community: The Taizé community is an ecumenical Christian monastic community in Taizé, Saome-et-Loire, Burgundy, France. It was founded in 1940 by Brother Roger Schütz and "Taizé prayer" refers to the prayer practice of this community. There is no preaching or teaching; instead, periods of contemplative silence are interspersed with simple, repeating chants set to music. Often these prayers take place by candlelight. You can experience Taizé online in a number of ways. A variety of podcasts are offered at www.taize.fr and every Saturday the evening prayer from Taizé is transmitted on Domradio, a Catholic radio station in Cologne. This recording can be downloaded at www.domradio.de.

Richard Rohr's Daily Meditations: These are free email reflections sent every day of the year. Each meditation features Richard Rohr and guest authors reflecting on a yearly theme, with each week's topic building on the previous week's topic. You can join at any time by signing up at www.cac.org.

Henri Nouwen Daily Meditation: Again, these are free email reflections sent daily throughout the year. Each one includes an excerpt from a wide range of Henri Nouwen's writings and a short, related Scripture reading. You can sign up at www.henrinouwen.org

Apps to Support Prayer: These days there seem to be apps for everything, and prayer is no exception. The following are apps you may wish to explore in supporting and deepening your prayer life:

- ~ *Centering Prayer*, offered by Contemplative Outreach, has various resources to support those interested in practising centering prayer (see the chapter "Praying with Silence"). You can choose opening and closing sounds, vary the duration of silence, and select opening and closing prayers from various categories including Psalms, Scripture and Thomas Keating.

- ~ *Reflect - Christian Mindfulness* houses a number of meditations grouped into different sections, including "Lectio Divina", "Imaginative Contemplation", "Quiet Prayer", and "Stress and Anxiety".

- ~ *Prayermate* allows you to enter your own categories for prayer (for example family, small group, and the Church) and shows you them as a series of index cards which you can swipe between as you pray.

- ~ *The Daily Prayer App* has prayers and Scripture passages for each day, arranged under "Morning Prayer", "Midday Prayer", "Evening Prayer" and "Late Evening Prayer".

CONTACT LIST PRAYER

Our contact lists provide useful prompts for intercessory prayer, reminding us to hold in love those placed in our lives. This practice invites you to establish your own rhythm of praying with your contact list or phone book but you could use any collection or list of names.

Practising

~ Breathe deeply and centre yourself in the awareness of being in the loving presence of God. A visualisation based on an image from the Psalms may be helpful here: for example, imagine being safely tucked under a wing (Psalm 91:4), or being held and comforted by a loving mother (Psalm 131:2).

~ Affirm your intent to acknowledge with love the needs and cares of those in your life. For example: God, I thank you for all those you have placed in my life. I thank you for who you have made them to be and I offer up their needs and their cares.

~ As you scroll through your contact list or move your finger down your phone book, say each person's name, inwardly or aloud.

~ Pause after each name and allow that person's face or voice or smile or laugh or tears to present themselves. If you reach a name of someone you have not seen or spoken to for a long time or have forgotten who they are, continue to take a moment to pause with their name. If you know the particular needs or concerns of this person, you can name these but try to be open to whatever happens as you pause with each name. You don't need to give God a comprehensive account of your knowledge of them unless this is something you particularly want to do. God already knows and loves them; your willingness to pray for them expresses your desire to be aligned or united with God's love for them.

~ Gently release that person to God's love. To help you do this, you may like to return to the centering image you used at the beginning.

~ Continue like this for as long as you like or feel led to do so.

~ End by asking God to accept your prayers or offer a word of blessing or simply return to your opening image and breathe deeply.

PRAYING WITH SOCIAL MEDIA

Part of practising a prayerful life is becoming more mindful of which things or activities numb, distract or diminish us and restricting these for the sake of our health and healing. For many people, this means reducing the amount of time spent in virtual spaces such as social media. These spaces are designed to manipulate brain chemistry, particularly the dopamine system, to keep us checking back and staying online. It would be simplistic, however, to label social media "bad" and it doesn't need to be removed from a prayerful life. This practice offers a way to shift how you approach social media and to turn scrolling into a prayerful practice.

Practising

~ Before logging onto social media, take a moment to pause and try to name your intentions. Why are you logging on at this time? What are you seeking in this space? How long do you intend to stay there? This isn't meant to be guilt-inducing but to situate habitual behaviours in honest self-reflection. If you find you're logging on out of compulsion or sense a nudge not to log onto social media, try to resist any urge to carry on regardless. You don't need to view this as a punishment or a sign that social media is inherently bad; instead, try to be open to receiving a nudge not to log on as a gift offered for your health and healing. See if you can accept that it might not be a good time for you to be connected in this way.

~ If you feel at peace to continue, take a moment to ground yourself in God's loving presence and to affirm that your identity does not lie in what you have, what you do or what others say about you but, rather, in being beloved. You can do this with words, bodily posture or with your breath. Ask for any particular grace you need in order to approach your limited time in this online space in a healthy way.

~ Deepen your breathing and slow your scrolling. Pause regularly to ask yourself:

> *What is the intention behind this post?*
> *Where do I see God or love in this person's life?*
> *How, if at all, is God or love inviting me to respond?*

~ Of course, what people post on social media is rarely an honest or accurate representation of what is actually happening in their lives, so receive what they offer lightly while remaining open to whatever insights may come.

~ Before you move on to the next post, gently offer each person to God perhaps by visualising them being enfolded in love or with a brief breath prayer (for example, by saying their name inwardly as you inhale and saying "be blessed" with your exhale).

~ If you notice that you are becoming anxious or insecure or angry, pause and, remembering God's presence with you, ask God to show you what is at the root of this. Do you feel as though something is missing? Is there a longing or hurt that is asking to be named and brought to God? Is it loneliness, a fear of rejection, a sense of being insignificant? Even if what you notice seems superficial, try to offer it honestly and without shame.

~ Consider ending your time on social media with this prayer or something similar: "Thank you for the gift of each of these people you have placed in my life. Help me to hold on to the knowledge and insight that is good and life-giving and to release what is draining and unnecessary. Please continue to work in me to heal and restore and to grow in me a generous, discerning and loving heart."

PRAYERFUL PAUSE

How many times do you unlock your phone out of boredom or compulsion? How often do you check your emails or social media without thinking? The following practice seeks to bring you back to the present and God's Presence by slowing you down and grounding you in what is real. It is based on a mindfulness practice and invites you to receive your senses as pathways to presence.

Practising

~ Remembering God's presence with you, slowly count down 5-4-3-2-1 and use the following prompts to connect you to what is happening right now.

~ Acknowledge five things that you can see. You can pick between big and small items. Go with whatever draws your eye.

~ Acknowledge four things that you can touch around you. Start with your own body (for example, your hair, hands or elbows), and then reach around you to feel objects nearby. You may also like to feel the ground beneath you.

~ Acknowledge three things you can hear. Instead of listening to your own thoughts or sounds in your body, try to listen for external noises. If you are somewhere quiet, listen for distant noises or for background noises such as a clock ticking or the hum of a computer.

~ Acknowledge two things that you can smell. This might be a challenge, especially if you are inside. Your clothing or furniture may provide some opportunities to connect with your sense of smell. You might also like to acknowledge the smell of the air around you.

~ Acknowledge one thing around you that you can taste. You don't have to eat anything new. Just become aware of what you already taste in your mouth. It could be your morning toothpaste or coffee, the sandwich you ate for lunch or the tea you drank this afternoon.

~ Wait in this moment with God, breathing deeply and listening inwardly.

TECHNOLOGY FAST

Even if you manage to establish healthy and/or prayerful ways to engage with technology, it's a good idea to take the occasional break. If this willingness to be interrupted flows from an intention to be more present to God within and around you, it carries the marks of prayer. Even if you find it difficult to maintain your fast, you will likely learn something valuable about yourself and your tendencies through the struggle. In fact, the aim of a fast is less to complete it successfully and more to recognise a deeper dependence on God and, usually, that dependence is revealed more through struggle than through success.

Practising

~ Identify the form of technology that you feel called to fast from. To what do you feel unhealthily attached? On what do you feel dependent? What drives your more compulsive behaviour? It could be checking emails, scrolling social media, listening to podcasts, searching the internet.

~ Consider how you can fast. If it's impossible for you to take a complete fast from checking emails, perhaps resolve to fast from checking them between certain hours or during certain days of the week.

~ Decide how long you would like to fast. Be realistic but try to push the limit of your comfort zone because it takes time to break habits. To offer a frame of reference, the traditional Lenten fast is 40 days, not including Sundays, of which there are 6.

~ Consider what you need to do to make the fast possible. What do you need to delete? Who do you need to tell? Do any other arrangements need to be made?

~ Begin your fast by setting an intention. In her book *How to Break Up with Your Phone*, Catherine Price offers the guiding question: "What do you want to pay attention to?"[3] Because this is a prayerful fast, your intention is to attend to God—but try to put some flesh on that basic intention. *What does it mean* for you to attend to God? How do you feel drawn? Try not to respond with what you think you should say and instead become aware of how God is inviting you. Remember that attending to God, others and to your deepest self are not opposed. Loving God, loving self and loving neighbour open onto each other. Where is God inviting you to place your attention?

~ Write down your intention somewhere you will see it when you might be tempted to break your fast. If you are fasting from checking your phone before bed, you could set as your lockscreen a photo of your intention or something that reminds you of your intention. Let this strengthen you during times of struggle.

~ If you break your fast, don't give up altogether. Acknowledge what has happened and be honest about why it happened but offer yourself loving kindness. Humour helps. Revisit your intention. Ask God for help.

~ When your fast is over, mark the event with something that signifies celebration to you. It could be a cake, a special drink, a balloon. Recognise that you are not celebrating your own strength of will (although you can, of course, acknowledge that!), but God's constant presence with you through the fast, regardless of your experience or perceived success. Reflect on what you have learnt from the fast and listen for how you feel drawn to proceed. Be honest about whether you need to return to whatever it was that you were fasting from. If you return to whatever you fasted from, consider how you might engage it

---

[3] Catherine Price, *How to Break-Up with your Phone* (California: Ten Speed Press, 2018), 82.

more healthily. Recognise that you will probably need to fast again and try to see that as a sign of humility rather than failure.

Praying with Silence

Imagine the scene: two people are sitting silently next to one another on a bench, at the edge of a park. You are standing behind them so you can't see their faces or expressions. As you let the scene develop in your mind, become aware of the quality of the silence. Is it neutral? Tense? Empty? Safe? Full? What does this tell you about the two people or their relationship, as you're imagining it? If the silence is tense, perhaps it's because they are strangers sitting unusually close to one another or perhaps because they are friends who have argued, their harsh words the punctuation of a hurt or resentful silence. If the silence is full, perhaps it's because they are each enjoying the sights and sounds of the park. Or, is it because they are deeply connected friends who don't need to speak to enjoy their time together? I wonder what your own experience of silence is or has been. When have you experienced silence as tense, empty, safe, or full?

Paying attention to the flavours of silence is important when trying to understand what it means to pray with silence. In our noisy world, it usually feels strange to just sit quietly. It can feel cold or empty, perhaps even frightening, as though there's nowhere to hide from our doubts and fears, our darker emotions, troubling thoughts and memories. If we feel repelled by the idea of praying with silence, it may be because we've had uncomfortable experiences of silence being a tense or lonely space to be avoided at all costs. Perhaps we feel that to be silent with God, or to experience God as silent with us, is to give, or be given, the cold shoulder. If, on the other hand, we're drawn to the idea of praying in silence, it may be because we've experienced, either for ourselves or through watching others, the safe, warm, full silence that comes from being with someone we truly trust, someone who has no agenda for us but who simply delights in our presence. While our experience of silent prayer can vary greatly, it's the capacity of silence to invite us into this safe or full presence that makes it so valuable and it's this welcoming and friendly silence that we are invited into when we pray without words. This silence doesn't indicate a failure of words but is a fullness out of which words come and to which they return. The invitation to pray in this sort of silence is an invitation to hold lightly our impulse to pin things down or get things right or receive answers, and instead, to open ourselves to receiving as already enough the mysterious yet constant presence of God. Praying with silence means naming as prayer our willingness to be lovingly present to God's loving presence.

In my experience, this can be both difficult and effortless, depending on the time or place. At some times and in some places the difference between earth and heaven seems to thin as though a veil is lifted and we see the holy in the ordinary. At these times and in these places my natural response is quiet awe, joy and reverence. Sometimes these thin times and places come already packaged as holy (for example, in cathedrals, at pilgrimage sites, during candlelit processions or on special days). Sometimes, though, heaven and earth seem to thin when we least expect it and it's only our deepest self that whispers to us "take notice." For me, this deeply known thinning happens particularly frequently in places of wild, natural beauty and early in the morning in the moment before I'm fully awake, but it can happen at any time—even when I'm washing dishes or sipping a cocktail.

Praying with silence doesn't indicate a failure of words but is a fullness out of which words come and to which they return.

At other times, entering into silent prayer is more challenging. When life feels like a conveyor belt with things happening in quick succession, pausing and becoming silent can feel like choosing to fall off and I worry I won't be able to get back on when needed. Sometimes there's just too much on my mind and, even if I manage to reach outer silence by unplugging from technology or going somewhere I can be alone, inner silence feels out of reach, my mind jumping around like a monkey between trees.

When silence is hard, it's tempting to give up on it—but I try not to because beneath that impulse to avoid is a deeper knowing that there is something in silence that I need more than ever. As writer and life coach Martha Beck writes, usually what is missing is nothing but the experience of letting go and becoming silent.[1] Since realising that my resistance to silence often comes in direct proportion to my need for it, I've found that I can use my inner chatter as a litmus test for my hunger for silence. Now, when my inner life is particularly noisy, I try to treat it like a flashing light on my soul's dashboard, alerting me to a need to slow down and make greater space for silent prayer.

Even when we do carve out time to be alone, the experience of silence can be multi-faceted. Many of my experiences testify to this but a day of silent retreat particularly stands out. That day my experience of silence truly spanned the spectrum. To begin with, the quiet was refreshing. I'd been feeling overwhelmed, and it was a relief to be freed from the need to speak or do. Time opened up and offered herself to be enjoyed. It was a gorgeously sunny summer's day and I sat outside and listened to the breeze in the trees and felt the grass between my fingers. I picked daisies and noticed the shape of their petals and the particular shade of pink that blushed their centres. I closed my eyes and surrendered to being present to wind, earth and sky. As the day wore on, though, unwanted thoughts began to pop into my head and unwelcome memories prompted painful emotion to bubble to the surface. I struggled to stay present to Presence; instead, I wanted to push away the questions, doubts and anxieties. I longed for the consoling distraction of conversation. Unsurprisingly, the more I tried to push away the unwanted thoughts and feelings the more they came. In the end I accepted I

---

[1] Martha Beck, *The Joy Diet: 10 Steps to a Happier Life* (London: Piatkus, 2003), 8.

couldn't get rid of them and instead tried to trust that my unease wasn't a failure and that God was still loving me just as much as ever. The day drew to a close with nothing fixed or resolved but I could, just about, notice a peace flowing beneath the noise of my thoughts.

Although my experience of silence varied greatly during the span of that day, I'm reluctant to label any part of it "good" or "bad". While the deep and peaceful period of silence was refreshing, I realise that there was still meaning and significance in the difficult period. The disturbing thoughts that bubbled up needed to do so. Not only did they alert me to what still needed grace and healing, they also provided me with the opportunity to practise radical trust in Love, beyond and beneath my feelings. Although it would have been pleasant to have felt happy and content all day long, that wouldn't have made the silence more successful. As the contemplative and monk Thomas Keating teaches, we can't judge our silence by our experience of it; it's much more important to pay attention to the fruit in our ordinary daily lives and this is usually a slow process.

Of the silent practice of centering prayer, Keating writes:

> "It is unwise to judge a prayer period on the basis of your psychological experience. Sometimes you may be bombarded with thoughts all during the time of prayer; yet it could be a very useful period of prayer. Your attention might have been much deeper than it seemed. In any case, you cannot make a valid judgement about how things are going on the basis of a single period of prayer. Instead you must look for the fruit in your ordinary daily life, after a month or two. If you are becoming more patient with others, more at ease with yourself, if you shout less often or less loudly at the children, feel less hurt if the family complains about your cooking—all these are signs that another set of values is beginning to operate in you."[2]

---

[2] Thomas Keating, *Open Mind, Open Heart* (New York: Continuum, 1986), 39.

Sometimes people are suspicious of silent prayer as a Christian spiritual practice assuming it's an Eastern practice opposed to sound biblical theology and that it needs to be resisted or, at the very least, treated with a good dose of skepticism. Underlying this seems to be two beliefs. First, that anything not clearly labelled as Christian has nothing to do with Christ and, second, that Scripture is opposed to silent prayer. I want to resist both. Following in the rich tradition of mystics and contemplatives, I understand the world as saturated with the glory of God and that Christ is mysteriously present in all that has been created. As such, all is enfolded in God and all peoples and places are sites of revelation. This sacramental view of all creation as holding together in Christ through and for whom all things were made takes seriously the rich theology of passages such as John 1 and Colossians 1:15-20. I also take seriously the many passages in Scripture that stress the value of silence, quietness and stillness. "Be still and know that I am God," reads Psalm 46:10. "In repentance and rest is your salvation, in quietness and trust is your strength," declares God in Isaiah 30:15. "I have calmed and quieted myself, I am like a weaned child with its mother; like a weaned child I am content," reflects the psalmist in Psalm 131:2.

Jesus' example and teaching also affirms the value of silent prayer. While he used words to pray in public, we're also told that Jesus would regularly withdraw to desolate places to pray.[3] The Gospels don't tell us how Jesus prayed during these alone times but the image of him in a desolate place is an image of solitude and silence. And although Jesus gave the disciples the prayer which we now call "the Lord's prayer" he also encouraged them to explore silent prayer, telling them to pray in secret by going into their room and shutting the door.[4] Since most people in Jesus' day didn't have their own bedroom or even a closet, shutting the door and praying

---

[3] Luke 5:16
[4] Matthew 6:6

to God in secret is best read in a figurative light as offering an image of going into one's inner self to pray to God in silence.

Scripture, then, encourages us to pray with both words and silence. They aren't opposed and praying with silence doesn't cheapen or replace word-filled prayer. Rather, silence liberates us from feeling bound by words. This is important because, however eloquent we might be, we can never fully articulate what we want to express. Anyone who has tried to write a love letter will know this, as will anyone who has tried to find the right words to comfort a bereaved friend or relative.

Silence liberates us from feeling bound by words.

When we're overjoyed or deeply troubled, it can be hard to find the words to express our intense feelings. But even in ordinary moments it can be hard to find the right words. One response is to worry less and to use the words we have and trust they're enough. Another approach is to use another person's words to give voice to our thoughts and feelings. Often, though, the best response is to allow the sense of insufficiency to guide us into still prayer. This is the approach St Paul favours in Romans 8.26 when he reassures his readers that the Spirit helps us in our weakness, and although we don't know what we ought to pray for, "the Spirit himself intercedes for us through wordless groans." Over time we learn to trust that our hearts speak for us in stillness, that the Spirit intercedes with groans, and that our willingness to be present and open is as precious as a thousand words.

Not only does silence liberate us in our prayer but it also completes our prayer. Prayer isn't only speaking to God but also listening to God. If our prayer lives are the sum total of the words we speak to God, when will we hear what God has to say to us? And yet silence isn't simply a container into which God pours thoughts and images and ideas. When we pray in silence, we don't sit alongside the silence waiting for God to deposit meaning which can then be retrieved; rather, we enter silence fully, immersing ourselves fully in its depths, releasing even the images and thoughts that we sense to be, in some way, from God. This *full immersion* experience of silence may seem counterintuitive and to cut against the desire to hear from God. But releasing what comes during silence doesn't mean rejecting what comes. Releasing images and thoughts means remaining open to God even as we begin to hear God speak. We trust that if what comes is from God we don't need to cling to it but can trust God to plant it deeper and deeper within us. As Keating explains, "Letting go of spiritual gifts is the best way to receive them. The more detached you are from them, the more you can receive or rather, the better you can receive."[5]

We also don't need to be worried we will forget what happens during silent prayer. In his book *A Taste of Silence*, Carl J. Arico asks the following questions to allay fears around forgetting:

> "Do you think that God only mentions things to you once? How many times has God had to repeat things to you, over and over again until finally you got it? If it is important it will be there for you after the prayer session."[6]

The advantage of this *full immersion* understanding to silence (over and against the container understanding) is that it allows us to enter the time with no preconceptions or expectations. We don't measure our time by what comes but bring ourselves into God's presence, trusting that we will be formed by it, even though it won't be according to our agenda or timeframes and perhaps not in ways we can easily verbalise or explain. We allow God's slow work to unfold within, with our role being only to hold open the space and maintain loving attention to God. This is a deeper listening for God, a listening not only with our sensory or intellectual faculties but with our whole selves.

---

[5] Thomas Keating, *Open Mind, Open Heart* (New York: Continuum, 1986), 76.
[6] Carl J. Arico, *A Taste of Silence: Centering Prayer and Contemplative Journey* (New York: Lantern Books, 2015), chap. 6, Kindle.

When it comes to silent prayer, those who tend towards quietness have a natural advantage but anyone who begins this practice is likely to struggle at the start. There's a difference between exterior and interior silence, and even if we find it easy to withdraw and attain exterior silence, it's quite another thing to establish interior silence. As soon as we quiet our surroundings, we become hyper-aware of the inner dialogue. Our minds jump around from one thought to another. It takes work to enter inner silence and remain there. This isn't the usual sort of work centred on striving and accomplishing but the work of unwinding and releasing, of learning to let go of doing, even the doing of thinking and feeling, so that we can find rest in the fullness of silence.

Part of this work of releasing and letting go is becoming gentle with distractions. If we try to shoot down distractions or force our way beneath them through a defiant act of will, our silent prayer will begin to feel like a battlefield and our vigilance will itself become a distraction. It's better to acknowledge distractions than to try to avoid having them. This acknowledging is part of the act of releasing; a letting be that also allows us to let go. It doesn't mean that we enter into an examination of distractions but that we recognise them for what they are—thoughts which we can choose to engage or not.[7] And when we release these thoughts, we don't reject them but offer them to God to be illuminated, purified and healed, honouring them without allowing them to take hold of us.

---

[7] To better understand this, it may be helpful to imagine yourself sitting on the ocean floor watching boats pass by above. You can remain in the deep while still acknowledging what is passing. It is only when you grab an anchor of one of the boats that you will begin to be pulled away. Similarly, you can acknowledge distractions from the depths of stillness without becoming caught up in them. See Cynthia Bourgeault, *Centering Prayer and Inner Awakening* (Lanham: Cowley Publications, 2004), 36-37.

Being distracted in prayer, then, isn't a sign of weakness or being unsuitable for silent prayer but rather, a sign that you are a human being seeking to attend to God even in the midst of the swirl of distraction. Silent prayer begins exactly at the point you decide to follow your longing for stillness, even when faced with myriad distractions. As Merton says, "If you have never had any distractions, you don't know how to pray."[8] What matters is not how distracted you are when you sit down to pray but that you sit down in the first place. It's our desire to be with God that is the heartbeat of our prayer and that being-with is possible no matter the storm of distraction. We can be comforted by the memory of God's "unfailing presence"[9] and reassured that God's presence does not depend on our thoughts; all is already enfolded and held.

> *Silent prayer begins exactly at the point we decide to follow our longing for stillness.*

The practices in this chapter offer a variety of gateways to silent prayer. As you begin to practise praying with silence, I recommend you begin with short periods and build up to longer stretches. Set a timer and begin with ten minutes. As you gradually learn to surrender into stillness and rest in God's presence, you'll be able to sustain longer periods of silence. This doesn't mean that silence will always be easy, but over time you'll notice you're more able to sit in the discomfort, trusting that God is there, and growing in confidence that God is healing and renewing you beneath the surface of your conscious awareness.

---

[8] Thomas Merton, *New Seeds of Contemplation* (New York: New Direction Books, 1961), 221.
[9] "No matter how distracted you may be, pray by peaceful, even perhaps inarticulate, efforts to centre your heart upon God, Who is present to you in spite of all that may be going through your mind. His presence does not depend on your thoughts of Him. He is unfailingly there; if He were not, you could not even exist. The memory of HIs unfailing presence is the surest anchor for our minds and hearts in the storm of distraction and temptation by which we must be purified." Ibid., 224.

For reflection

Do you crave or dread silence and stillness?

What are the barriers to silence and stillness in your life?

How might words sometimes block your prayer?

Which images or feelings might be hardest to release in silent prayer?

OPEN HANDS PRAYER

Praying with silence need not be complicated. This practice, adapted from an article in *Connections* (the Spiritual Directors International magazine), reminds us that praying with silence requires only our willingness to be open and present. It may help you to prepare for more extended periods of silent prayer.

This simple practice works best outside, even without sunlight, but can be practised anywhere, including indoors. Your task is only to open your hands. There is no grasping for objects or fears or worries. By opening your hands and waiting without specific expectation, you may be surprised by how your heart, mind, and spirit open to receive the blessings that are already here and waiting for you.

Practising

~ Leave your phone inside.

~ Go outside.

~ Open your hands.

~ Fill with sunlight (or moonlight).

~ Listen as you wait for nothing in particular.

TWO DOWN, TWO UP

This simple practice uses bodily posture to guide silent prayer. It is inspired by a more extended meditation exercise found in Richard Foster's book *Celebration of Discipline*.[10] This version of Foster's "Palms Down, Palms Up" practice may appeal to those intrigued yet intimidated by silent prayer because it only involves four minutes of silence; two minutes for sitting with palms facing down and two minutes for sitting with palms facing up. It can be practised any time but is particularly helpful as a re-centering practice during transitions in the day or week.

Practising

~ Before you begin, decide how you will keep time. You might like to set a timer for two minutes but you will need to interrupt your silence to reset it. Consider setting two timers with fixed alarm

---

[10] Richard Foster, *Celebration of Discipline: The Path to Spiritual Growth* (London: Hodder and Stoughton, 2008), 30-31.

sounds, one for two minutes and one for four minutes. This way, you won't need to break your silence.

~ Close your eyes and take a deep breath. Let your body know it is safe to relax.

~ Place your palms down on your knees or on your chair. This is a sign of your willingness to release.

~ For two minutes, release whatever you notice as it bubbles to the surface of conscious awareness. Gently let go of any thoughts, images or feelings. Release any judgement that comes with anything that arises.

~ After two minutes, slowly turn your palms to face up. This is a sign of your willingness to receive.

~ For two minutes, sit with your openness to receive. If this is difficult and you feel distracted or stuck in releasing mode, let your palms be a sign of your willingness to try to be open to receive. Receive whatever comes without clinging to it so that you can continue to receive for the full two minutes.

~ When four minutes are up, bring your palms together and say Amen. Stay in that gathered posture for as long as you would like.

SILENT SETTLING PRAYER

Even when we feel drawn to silence, it can be difficult to know what to do with our busy minds. It can be tempting to try to overcome thoughts but this is an inherently violent approach that tends to keep us at the surface of ourselves. This practice offers a pathway for moving beneath rather than through, around or above thoughts. It uses the image of a pebble dropping into water to guide your inner movement as you settle into God's indwelling presence.

Practising
~ Sit down and, keeping your back straight but free, begin quieting your mind and your body by taking a few relaxing, deep breaths. Close your eyes if you wish.

~ Without judgement, resistance or analysis, notice what is at the surface of your awareness (for example, thoughts, feelings and bodily sensations).

~ Allowing the noisy surface of yourself to remain, see if you can let your awareness or energy move towards your centre. You are not trying to ignore or deny the thoughts, feelings or bodily sensations, you are simply moving beneath them, like a pebble sinking beneath choppy waves into the still and silent depths.

~ If you notice yourself analysing what is happening or becoming caught up in a thought process, you are floating back to the surface. Be gentle with yourself and your thoughts. Let them be while allowing your awareness to, once again, sink deeper towards your centre.

~ As you draw near to your hushed centre where God dwells as the source and ground of your being, you may notice a sensation of settling, deepening or quieting. Release this noticing, as you would any other, allowing yourself to sink deeper into your inmost being where you rest in God and God rests in you.

~ Remain here as long as you like.

251

~ Allow time to float back to the surface of words and thoughts, moving slowly and taking with you the unspeakable wisdom of the silent depths.

CENTERING PRAYER

The practice of centering prayer was developed in the 1970s and 1980s by the Trappist monk, Thomas Keating, partly in response to the surge of popularity of Eastern meditation. Recognising that what many were seeking in Buddhism was already present and practised in Christian monasticism, he set about making contemplative practices more widely accessible. As Keating emphasised, centering prayer is not a program for achieving union with God through our own effort but, rather, a method of consenting to the presence of God. Through this consenting, we are readied to receive the freely given gift of contemplation in which the soul enjoys union with God. Although Keating's formulation of the practice was new, centering prayer builds on ancient practices of silent, contemplative prayer stretching back to fourth century desert monasticism and to Jesus' own words about going to one's "inner room" to pray. For more on the origins and intentions of centering prayer, see Keating's *Open Mind, Open Heart* and Cynthia Bourgeault's *Centering Prayer and Inner Awakening*.

Practising
~ Decide how long you will spend in silence. Teachers of centering prayer generally recommend two twenty minute "sits" per day, one early in the morning and one later in the day or evening. You are, however, welcome to start out slowly, perhaps with initial prayer periods lasting five to ten minutes. See if you can let go of

a goal and trust that your consent to be present, or try to be present, is enough.

~ Decide how you will keep time. Contemplative Outreach offers a centering prayer app that allows you to choose the duration of your sit and what sound will begin and end your time in silence.

~ Sit in an upright, attentive posture in a way that allows for an erect spine and open heart. Place your hands in your lap.

~ Gently close your eyes and bring to mind a sacred word, image or breath as your symbol to consent to the presence and action of God within you. Your sacred symbol is intended to be the same every time you pray. It helps to ground you in the present moment, allowing you to give your undivided, loving, yielded attention to God. Some suggestions include "Father", "Mother", "Jesus", "Spirit", "Love", "Peace", "Release", "Open", and "Present". If you like, you can spend a few minutes silently waiting for a word to offer itself to you but don't get too hung up on the exact word. You won't be meditating on this word and its meaning but offering it to yourself as a reminder of your intent to be present. For this reason, some people find it unhelpful to choose a word that is heavily laden with meaning.

~ Silently, with eyes closed, recall your sacred symbol to begin your prayer. As you notice your thoughts, return to your sacred word and your intent to be present. In this way, you bring yourself "back into alignment with your original intention...to maintain that bare, formless openness to God."[11]

~ When you notice thoughts, don't try to violently shoot them down with your sacred symbol. Instead, let them be and return, ever so gently, to your sacred symbol. You aren't trying to avoid having

---

[11] Cynthia Bourgeault, *Centering Prayer and Inner Awakening* (Lanham: Cowley Publications, 2004), 23.

thoughts but to avoid being hooked or caught up in them. Do this as often as thoughts arise. Don't be disheartened if you find yourself flooded with thoughts: each one offers an invitation to return to your intention.[12]

~ If you notice bodily sensations (for example heaviness in your hands or feet), gently release this, too. Release all noticings, allowing yourself to sink further into the present and openness to God's Presence.

~ If a vision or word of wisdom comes to you, release this, too. You don't need to grasp onto it because if it is important for you to remember, you will remember it; if it is from God, it will return.

~ When your prayer period is over, transition slowly from your prayer practice to your active life. It's likely that the only parts of the sit you'll remember are the distractions but, as Cynthia Bourgeault writes, these times "have been counterbalanced by times of deep resting at your depths," so try to honour the time you spent in silence by choosing not to judge or dismiss it.[13]

How will I know if I'm doing it right?

As many centering prayer teachers will tell you, the only way to 'fail' at this practice is to get up and walk out. As long as you are sitting and trying to return to your sacred word when thoughts arise, you are practising centering prayer. Some sits will be full of

---

[12] "In one of the very earliest training workshops led by Father Thomas Keating himself, a nun tried out her first twenty-minute taste of Centering Prayer and then lamented, 'Oh Father Thomas, I'm such a failure at this prayer. In twenty minutes I've had ten thousand thoughts!' 'How lovely,' responded Keating, without missing a beat. 'Ten thousand opportunities to return to God.'" Cynthia Bourgeault, *The Heart of Centering Prayer and Non-Dual Spirituality*, (Boulder: Shambhala, 2016), 13.
[13] Ibid., 29.

distractions and afterwards it'll feel as though you've spent the whole time noticing thoughts and returning to your intent to be present. Other times you may have moved beyond or beneath distractions and be unsure whether you have been asleep or not. Both are part of the experience of centering prayer. Even during sits filled with thoughts, there will be fleeting moments of deep resting where you do sink into being wholly present to God. While you won't be able to remember or perceive these directly, you may retain some "residual memory" of them in the way of "an explicable sense of refreshment, and sometimes a vivid sense of having been tugged down deep into your own heart, or having sat at the edge of an incredible intimacy and tenderness."[14]

It's important, however, that you don't try to measure the value or 'success' of your time in silence based on your experience of it or what you remember. Time and again, Keating explained that the real fruits of centering prayer are found in daily life. Noticing an increase in your ability to be present, forgiving and flexible is a sign that you are spending time in the mysterious, silent depths and are being transformed from the inside out.

WELCOMING PRAYER

The welcoming prayer isn't a silent prayer but is included here because of its close connection with centering prayer. It offers a way to remain centered in God's presence all day long, whatever your

---

[14] Ibid., 30.

situation or circumstances. As Cynthia Bourgeault explains, the welcoming prayer is a "powerful path for connecting the inner consent of Centering Prayer with the outer requirement of unconditional presence in daily life."[15]

The original version of the welcoming prayer was formulated in the 1980s by Mary Mrozowski, one of the founders of Contemplative Outreach, an ecumenical organisation dedicated to sharing the practice of centering prayer. Influenced by the 17th century French spiritual classic *Abandonment to Divine Providence* by Jean-Pierre de Caussade as well as Keating's teachings and her own lived experience, Mrozowski developed the welcoming prayer as a practice of radical love. By encouraging us to welcome all of life while letting go of the impulse to grasp, dominate or control, this practice teaches us how to open-heartedly consent to God's action and presence in daily life.

The following version of the practice is adapted from Cynthia Bourgeault's description of the method in her book *Centering Prayer and Inner Awakening* and the quotations are hers.[16]

Practising

~ Focus and sink in.

~ Check in with your body. Where are there sensations? Is there stress or tension? Is there pain?

~ Allow thoughts and emotions free reign. Where is the energy? Give it all of your attention. Move with it freely.

---

[15] Quoted in 'An Introduction to the Welcoming Prayer,' an article produced by Contemplative Outreach.
[16] For more on the welcoming prayer and Mary Mrozowski, see www.contemplativeoutreach.org and www.marymrozowski.com

~ Sink into whatever your mind or body presents as though sinking into a Jacuzzi or warm bath. Most importantly: "Don't try to change anything. Just stay present."[17]

Welcome.

~ Wherever you are drawn in your mind or body create an atmosphere of "inner hospitality" by saying, "Welcome, welcome." If you notice anger, say: "Welcome, anger." If you notice pain, say: "Welcome, pain." This expresses your willingness to feel whatever is presented and not to run away from it or try to repress or avoid it. This enacts your consent to be unconditionally present and to be with God now, whatever may be happening. This doesn't mean you are acquiescing with all situations but, rather, that you are remaining aligned with your "magnetic center, the seat of your inner observer, through which Divine Being can flow to you."[18]

~ Stay with your feelings, welcoming them as they present themselves.

~ Before moving to the final step, allow yourself plenty of time to go back and forth between focusing and welcoming. This is the "real work" of the Welcoming Prayer that allows the "knot" of feeling to "dissolve of its own accord."[19]

Let go. (There are two ways to do this.)

~ One way is to offer a statement of intent as a way of "inwardly [waving] farewell to the emotion as it

---

[17] Cynthia Bourgeault, *Centering Prayer and Inner Awakening* (Lanham: Cowley Publications, 2004), 143.
[18] Ibid., 146.
[19] Ibid., 147.

starts to recede."[20] For example, you could say: "I let go of anger/ pain/ fear/ envy/ etc." or "I give my anger/ pain/ fear/ envy/ etc. to God."

~ The other way is less about bidding farewell to the emotion or sensation and more about bidding farewell to the desire to impulsively respond to it. You may like to use the following statements of intent, based on a formula favoured by Mary Mrozowski:

"I let go of my desire for security and survival."

"I let go of my desire for affection and esteem."

"I let go of my desire for power and control."

"I let go of my desire to change the situation/ feeling/ emotion/ sensation/ thought."

"I embrace the moment as it is."

~ These statements affirm a willingness to release the fear-driven false-self programs to protect or insulate self by accruing power, possessions and approval. By releasing these programs, you "send a strong message to the unconscious"[21] and choose to remain fully present to God in what is actually happening right now for as long as it lasts.

---

[20] Ibid., 147.
[21] Ibid., 147.

SCRIPTURAL MEDITATION AS A GATEWAY TO SILENT PRAYER

The final stage of the ancient practice of *lectio divina* is contemplation, in which the soul moves beyond words and meditation into quiet awareness and finds its rest in God. This final step is mysterious and Spirit-guided because it involves a deep letting-go. This practice offers a way to ease into that letting-go by allowing meditation to deepen as words slowly slip away. The verses suggested below lend themselves particularly well to this practice but you could try it with other verses too, especially those that begin with a word that is pregnant with meaning or significance.

Practising

~ Take some time to settle yourself in the time and place you find yourself. Slow and deepen your breathing.

~ Repeat, inwardly or aloud Psalm 46.10: "Be still and know that I am God."

~ Pause and allow the words to reverberate and then settle. Notice what stands out to you. Offer that noticing by gently releasing it and returning to stillness.

~ Repeat, inwardly or aloud, "Be still and know that I AM..."

~ Again, pause, notice and release.

~ Repeat, inwardly or aloud, "Be still and know..."

~ Pause, notice and release.

~ Repeat, inwardly or aloud, "Be still..."

~ Pause, notice and release.

~ Repeat, inwardly or aloud, "Be..."

~ Pause, notice and release.

~ Linger in the stillness.

~ If you find yourself becoming caught up in thoughts, repeat the word, "Be..." as a way to guide yourself back into stillness.

Peace meditation
An adaptation of this practice involves repeating John 14.27 in a similar way:

~ "Peace I leave with you; my peace I give you... Do not let your hearts be troubled and do not be afraid."

~ "Peace I leave with you; my peace I give you.... Do not let your hearts be troubled..."

~ "Peace I leave with you; my peace I give you..."

~ "Peace I leave with you..."

~ "Peace I leave..."

~ "Peace..."

Conclusion: Praying as Yourself

Let's return a final time to the lakeside scene with which we began. Cast your eyes again over the lake front as you feel the refreshing breeze on your warm skin. Notice the way the water twinkles in the sunlight and listen to the waves lapping the shore. See the children running and laughing; the man swimming; the woman floating. Catch a glimpse of the couple's entwined hands as they walk along the shoreline, follow the ball tossed between the teenagers and notice the vulnerability of the woman who sits at the water's edge as she allows the water to lap at her legs.

Now, imagine the ten ways of praying as different ways of being in and by the lake. Slowly cast your eyes down the list of chapters and notice any inward response.

Praying with Scripture
Praying with Nature
Praying with Our Intellects
Praying with Our Bodies
Praying with the Story of Our Lives
Praying with and for Others
Praying with Our Imaginations
Praying with Our Creativity
Praying with Technology
Praying with Silence

Which of these ways of praying draws your attention? Do any prompt an inward smile? Did any feel natural or easy? Did any feel challenging? Did anything surprise you? Do you remember being particularly moved by any of them or the practices they contained? Is there anything you'd like to revisit?

Take some time to notice your responses but don't force your thinking. Allow these questions to linger and be attentive to the thoughts, memories and feelings that may present themselves over the course of the coming minutes, hours and days. There is no rush.

My intention in offering the practices contained within this book has been to swing wide the doors of prayer. My hope is that you will feel invited to pray in freedom, to play in the living water always and abundantly available to you. Perhaps, though, in reviewing the ways of praying we have explored, you find yourself a little overwhelmed. Perhaps it feels like too much choice. Perhaps the variety seems unnecessarily to complicate prayer.

If any of this rings true, please let me offer a complementary image for prayer, one that might help to alleviate any feeling of overwhelm as you review the practices we have explored.

It is the image of an inner fire.

I borrow this image from Luigi Gioia who, in his book *Say it to God*, explains how this image transformed his own understanding of prayer. He recalls how, as a teenager, his faith had come alive and he was trying to work in some prayer time each day. Distracted by his siblings, he became increasingly impatient and, later, angry. At the end of a particularly frustrating week, he went to speak to a Benedictine monk. The monk listened attentively and then responded by telling him the story of a Christian who had been held in a tiny, overcrowded cell in Vietnam during a time of persecution.

Even if the fire burns low or even appears to go out, the spark remains within, waiting to be reignited.

When he was released, many years later, this monk said that nothing in the prison, not even the noise, discomfort or shouting had distracted him from prayer. Rather, it had been the fuel for his prayer, a medium and not an obstacle.

Gioia then remembers the Benedictine monk telling him, "The test that your prayer is authentic is learning how to turn everything into prayer. Any scrap of wood is good to feed fire."[1]

I love this image of our prayer life as a fire that we can keep going by feeding any scrap of wood. It reminds me that in prayer, as in fire tending, too much time analysing what should go in is detrimental to the blazing of the fire. To keep the fire going all we need to do is add something and do so regularly. While I encourage you to take time to review the practices, to notice your response to them and to listen for God's invitation, don't be afraid to just make a start and see what happens. There are no rules and no grades in prayer. You cannot get it wrong. And even if the fire burns low or even appears to go out, the spark remains within, waiting to be reignited. This spark is given, not earned. It's a gift and as long as we remain God's creatures (which, of course, we will forever be) the spark of prayer can never be extinguished. Our only choices are whether to blow on the spark until it ignites and, when ignited, whether we will continue to feed and stoke the fire.

I think of these practices as ways to play in living water and also as scraps of wood to ignite the inner spark and feed the fire. They are scraps that you may not have noticed lying about you, scraps that you don't need to conjure or find but are placed into your open arms. I offer them to you as others have offered them to me: together, we are a great chain of pray-ers who seek fuel for their inner fires. I pass them on to you as one beginner to another.

And yet, although I hope you have found and will continue to find something amongst these practices to feed the fire of your prayer life, these particular scraps are not the only scraps. These chapters must not, then, be treated as checklists of must-try activities. Beyond giving you ideas to nurture your prayer life, my intention has been to encourage and inspire your own personal forms of prayer. As well as scraps to feed the fire of our prayer, I think of these practices as exercises designed to expand your range of vision so that you will more easily see the scraps of wood all around you. And

---

[1] Luigi Gioia, *Say it to God: In Search of Prayer* (London: Bloomsbury, 2017), 3.

not only scraps, but a whole forest ready and waiting to be turned into food for your spiritual fire. This is important because we don't learn to pray by learning to make our prayer life resemble that of others. We learn to pray by learning how to be more fully ourselves in prayer. This doesn't mean forcing ourselves to look or sound different from others but stepping into the freedom of no longer needing to perform and beginning simply where we are. This enables us to let go of measuring and comparing, instead delighting in the prayer of others and in our own prayer as we recognise and value the similarities and the differences as a delightful consequence of us all being both similar and different to one another.

> We learn to pray by learning how to be more fully ourselves in prayer.

As we reach our end, I want to move beyond and beneath metaphors and practices and affirm a truth that I hope has been the golden thread through all the preceding pages: the truth that God is already here and you are already loved. God isn't a distant figure out-there who needs to be placated or impressed but is present to you as intimately as a lover is present to their beloved.

Your identity as beloved is what grounds prayer and makes it safe to be playful in prayer. You can't earn the right to come before God but are invited to respond to an already given presence. By responding to God in prayer you live into your identity as beloved and, in time, your experience of God's love will expand and deepen. This experience is personal and intimate as well as expansive and inclusive. It is for you and it is for everyone. And while your experience of God's love may shift over time, it will always be the same love that holds you. Allowing yourself to be loved ever more deeply by God is the gift and goal of prayer. To desire this love isn't selfish but the only pathway to real transformation and service. Our efforts will help us on our way but will not alone suffice. Only Love can awaken us to our true calling to be loving people, ready and willing to share what we continue to receive.

My closing prayer for you, then, is that you may dare to believe that the good news of God's love is really true. And not only true in an abstract sense but true for *you* whoever you are, wherever you are, whatever you have done, whatever your doubts or pain or fear. Come before God honestly, bring whatever you have, and let God love you.

A Blessing for You

Child of God, may you play in God's living water.
May you be yourself.
You are free to come as you are;
bring your words and silence,
your body, thoughts and feelings,
your memories and imagination,
your creativity and your wounds.
You can take off your mask:
let God see you, smile upon you, and love you.
Soak in God's gaze and linger long enough
to be awakened by love into love.

Child of God,
may you play
before God,
with God,
in God.

May you allow the fire within to dance.
Here you can play with fire.
Tend the spark and stoke the flames,
dance around the light burning within.

Child of God,
may the refreshment of God's water,

and the warmth of God's fire
guide you home into love.
Return again and again
so that your life is a returning to love
and you are always at home.

Acknowledgements

This project would never have got started, much less finished, without the help and encouragement of many friends. Together you've offered just the right amount of comfort, encouragement, excitement, reassurance, insistence and practical assistance to keep me going. By helping me to stay present to the unfolding process you have helped this work to remain prayerful from beginning to end. Looking back, God's help and yours are practically indistinguishable, so wonderfully have you loved me. Whatever fruit this bears is as much yours as it is mine.

To Dave Van Winkle - this project began with your suggestion that I write a leaflet about prayer that could be given to anyone "no matter their experience of prayer or church or life." At the time I laughed and said I had no idea what that leaflet would look like, but it turned out to be an excellent prompt. I'm not sure if this answers the call but here's my attempt! Thank you for the invitation to start and for believing I could do it.

So many others from Missio Dei Uptown, Chicago encouraged me in the early stages of writing. To Amyie Kao, Jenny Jones, Heidi Koval, Danielle Chu, Lauren Gamache, Caroline Wright, Eve Haycock, Amy White, Jen Loboda, Kristie Walstrum, Jen Goolsby, Ashley Chitwood and all those I shared my life and words with (you know who you are)—you helped me to believe that there was an audience for my writing and these practices. Thank you, in particular, for reading an early draft and exploring the practices with me. I will treasure the memory of those group spiritual direction times.

There are others in the US who kept me going and who also have my sincere thanks. To Lindsey Moon, Emily Todor, Amber Jipp,

Karin Holsinger, Sister Mary Jane and countless more—your excitement and kindness helped to prevent me from shrinking away from the work. So many of our conversations tended my soul and the inner fire of my prayer. I miss you all.

To Cohort 15 and all those we encountered through the C. John Weborg Center for Spiritual Direction—the journey from seed of idea to completed book is entwined with our journey. Together we went on an adventure of prayer, exploring new ways to enjoy God. I can't read this finished piece without thinking of you all. Ken Lund, it was your table of retreat materials that inspired the vision of the lake with which this book begins. Thank you for sharing them freely.

To Amy Knorr and Troy Cady—you deserve an extra special thank you. Not only did you give me the practical help to convert a messy manuscript into a book, you enfolded me in love and prayer, and strengthened me when I needed it most. I love working with you both because I always feel able to be completely myself. That is a gift you offer to many besides me.

In the UK I have many people to thank, too. To my parents and sisters and extended family (particularly my Uncle Tim)—your enthusiasm and your questions motivated me to keep going. Thank you for being my cheerleaders, in this and in so many other things.

To many British friends, including Matt Bullimore, Fiona Koefoed-Jespersen, Hazel Erskine, Dalia El-Saleh and Faith Dwight—thank you for clarifying conversations that helped this book to take shape. To Matt I offer an additional thank you for reading a draft and being so generous and helpful with your comments.

To Leslie Griffiths—for all your kind emails and your generous foreword, thank you. I'm delighted you think that this is "not a guilt-inducing book."

To the major publishing house who turned down this project because I didn't have a large enough platform—thank you. Through your no I found freedom to say yes to a deeper longing for a quieter, more hidden life that overflows in ways I may not always know.

To my directees and my friends in the Black Barn—when I've struggled to picture who I'm writing this for, your lovely faces come to me. I hope that you'll find something here to nourish you or which you might like to explore together. It is my honour and joy to accompany you on your journey.

To my husband, Tom—I wouldn't be able to do this work without your constant support and help. Thank you for the ways you've enabled me to find the space and quiet I needed to write this thing. Thank you also for your endless patience, forgiveness and love.

To my children, Henry and Phoebe—I imagine your surprise when you see your names here but of course you get the final thanks. You have taught me more about how to give and receive love than anyone else in the world. Parenting you has been a deep yes to God. You already know how to pray as yourselves, but I hope you'll find some fun things in here to try, either now or in the future. Remember: my love is just a tiny taste of God's love and so there is nothing for you to fear. Thank you for teaching me so much about play and prayer and love and God and how to be myself. I promise to keep reminding you of what you already know.

Bibliography

Anderson, Robert and Johann M. Moser, eds. *The Aquinas Prayer Book: The Prayers and Hymns of St Thomas Aquinas*. Nashua, NH: Sophia Institute Press, 2000.

Anselm of Canterbury. *Anselm of Canterbury: The Major Works*, edited by Brian Davies and G.R. Evans. Oxford: Oxford University Press, 1998.

Aquinas, Thomas. *Summa Theologiae*. newadvent.org/summa/.

Arico, Carl J. *A Taste of Silence: Centering Prayer and Contemplative Journey*. New York: Lantern Books, 2015. Kindle.

Aristotle. *Nichomachean Ethics*. Oxford: Oxford University Press, 2009.

Artress, Lauren. *Walking a Sacred Path*. New York: Riverhead, 2006.

Au, Wilke. *The Enduring Heart: Spirituality for the Long Haul*. Mahwah: Paulist Press, 2000.

Augustine of Hippo. *Confessions*. London: Penguin, 1961.

-----*The Essential Augustine*. Translated by Vernon Bourke. Indianapolis: Hackett, 1974.

-----*Of True Religion*. Washington, DC: Regnery Gateway: 1991.

Beck, T. David. *Luminous: Living the Presence and Power of Jesus*. Downers Grove: InterVarsity Press, 2013.

Beck, Martha. *The Joy Diet: 10 Steps to a Happier Life*. London: Piatkus, 2003.

Blythe, Teresa A. *50 Ways to Pray: Practices from Many Traditions and Times*. Nashville: Abingdon Press, 2006.

Bonhoeffer, Dietrich. *Psalms: The Prayer Book of the Bible*. Minneapolis: Augsburg, 1970.

Bourgeault, Cynthia. *Centering Prayer and Inner Awakening*. Lanham: Cowley Publications, 2004.

-----*The Heart of Centering Prayer and Non-Dual Spirituality.* Boulder: Shambhala, 2016.

Brown Taylor, Barbara. *Learning to Walk in the Dark: Because God Often Shows Up at Night.* London: HarperOne, 2015.

Brueggemann, Walter. *Praying the Psalms: Engaging Scripture and the Life of the Spirit.* Eugene, OR: Cascade Books, 2007.

Cady, Troy B. *Playful: Play as a Pathway to Personal and Relational Vitality.* Chicago: independently published, 2019.

Calvin, John. *Commentary on the Book of Psalms.* Grand Rapids, MI: William B. Eerdmans Publishing Co., 1949.

Campbell, Peter A. and Edwin M. McMahon. *BioSpirituality: Focusing as a Way to Grow.* Chicago: Loyola, 1985.

Casey, Michael. *Sacred Reading: The Ancient Art of Lectio Divina.* Liguori, MO: Triumph Books, 1996.

Cepero, Helen. *Journaling as a Spiritual Practice.* Downers Grove: InterVarsity Press, 2008.

Collins, Francis. *Language of God: A Scientist Presents Evidence for Belief.* New York: Free Press, 2007.

Community of Jesus, The. *The Little Book of Hours: Praying with the Community of Jesus.* Brewster, MA: Paraclete Press, 2007.

Evans, Rachel Held and Matthew Paul Turner. *What is God Like?* Danvers, MA: Convergent, 2021.

Farrer, Lauralee. *Praying the Hours in Ordinary Life.* Eugene, OR: Cascade Books, 2010.

Fleming, David L. *What is Ignatian Spirituality?* Chicago: Loyola Press, 2008.

Foster, Kenelm. *The Life of St Thomas Aquinas.* London: Longman, 1959.

Foster, Richard. *Celebration of Discipline: The Path to Spiritual Growth.* London: Hodder and Stoughton, 2008.

Gioia, Luigi. *Say it to God: In Search of Prayer.* London: Bloomsbury, 2017.

Guite, Malcolm. *David's Crown: Sounding the Psalms.* Norwich: Canterbury Press, 2021.

Hall, Thelma. *Too Deep for Words: Rediscovering Lectio Divina.* Mahwah: Paulist Press, 1988.

Hamm, Dennis. "Rummaging for God: Praying Backwards through Your Day." *America Magazine*, May 14, 1994.

Harter, Michael, ed. *Hearts on Fire: Praying with Jesuits.* Chicago: Loyola University Press, 2005.

Ignatius of Loyola. *Spiritual Exercises and Selected Works.* Mahwah: Paulist Press, 1991.

Jones, Sally Lloyd. *The Jesus Storybook Bible.* Grand Rapids: Zonderkidz, 2007.

Julian of Norwich. *Revelations of Divine Love.* London: Penguin, 1998.

Keating, Thomas. *Open Mind, Open Heart.* New York: Continuum, 1986.

Lamott, Ann. *Plan B: Further Thoughts on Faith.* Hull: Riverhead Books, 2006.

Lewis, C. S. *The Last Battle.* London: HarperCollins, 2015.

Linn, Matthew, Sheila Fabricant Linn and Francisco Miranda. *Sleeping with Bread: Holding What Gives You Life.* Mahwah: Paulist Press, 1995.

Macbeth, Sybil. *Praying in Color: Drawing a New Path to God.* Orleans: Paraclete Press, 2007.

McCabe, Herbert. *God, Christ and Us.* London: Bloomsbury, 2005.

-----*God Matters.* London: Continuum, 1987.

McGrath, Alistair. "Loving God with Heart and Mind." *Knowing and Doing*, Winter 2002. cslewisinstitue.org.

-----"Breaking the science-atheism bond." *Science and Spirit Magazine.* Accessed 4 April, 2022. https://www.beliefnet.com/news/science-religion/2005/08/breaking-the-science-atheism-bond.aspx

McHugh, Adam S. *The Listening Life: Embracing Attentiveness in a World of Distraction.* Downers Grove, IL: IVP Books, 2015.

Merton, Thomas. *Conjectures of a Guilty Bystander.* New York: Doubleday, 1966.

-----*New Seeds of Contemplation.* New York: New Direction Books, 1961.

Montgomery, L. M. *Anne of Green Gables.* New York: Barnes and Noble, 2016.

Mulholland, M. Robert, Jr. *Shaped by the Word: The Power of Scripture in Spiritual Formation.* Nashville: Upper Room, 1985.

Murray, Paul. *Aquinas at Prayer: The Bible, Mysticism and Poetry.* London: Bloomsbury, 2013.

Nouwen, Henri. *Behold the Beauty of the Lord.* Notre Dame: Ave Maria, 2007.

-----*Here and Now: Living in the Spirit.* New York: The Crossroad Publishing Company, 1994.

-----*Life of the Beloved: Spiritual Living in a Secular World.* New York: The Crossroad Publishing Company, 1992.

-----*Spiritual Formation: Following the Movements of the Spirit.* London: SPCK, 2011.

---*The Way of the Heart: Connecting with God Through Prayer, Wisdom and Silence.* New York: Ballantine, 1983.

-----*With Open Hands.* Notre Dame: Ave Maria, 2006.

O'Donohue, John. *Anam Cara: Spiritual Wisdom from the Celtic World.* London: Bantam, 1999.

-----*The Four Elements: Reflections on Nature.* London: Transworld Ireland, 2012.

Paintner, Christine Valters. *The Artist's Rule: Nurturing Your Creative Soul with Monastic Wisdom.* Notre Dame: Sorin Books, 2011.

-----*Lectio Divina, the Sacred Art: Transforming Words and Images into Heart-Centered Prayer.* Woodstock, VT: Skylight Paths Publishing, 2011.

-----and Betsey Beckman. *Awakening the Creative Spirit: Bringing the Arts to Spiritual Direction.* Harrisburg, PA: Morehouse Publishing, 2010.

Peterson, Eugene, H. *Answering God: The Psalms as Tools for Prayer.* New York: Harper One, 1989.

Price, Catherine. *How to Break-Up With Your Phone*. California: Ten Speed Press, 2018.

Roberts, Elizabeth and Elias Amidon, eds. *Earth Prayers: 365 Prayers, Poems, and Invocations from Around the World*. San Francisco: HarperOne, 2009.

Rohr, Richard. *The Divine Dance: The Trinity and your Transformation*. New Kensington, PA: Whitaker House, 2016.

-----*Eager to Love: The Alternative Way of St Francis of Assisi*. London: Hodder and Stoughton, 2014.

-----*Falling Upwards: A Spirituality for the Two Halves of Life*. London: SPCK, 2012.

-----*The Naked Now: Learning to See as the Mystics See*. New York: The Crossroad Publishing Company, 2009.

Silf, Margaret. *Inner Compass: An Invitation to Ignatian Spirituality*. Chicago: Loyola Press, 1999.

Spiritual Directors International. *Connections*. January 25, 2018.

Teresa of Calcutta and Brian Kolodiejchuk. *Come Be My Light: The Revealing Private Writings of the Nobel Peace Prize Winner*. London: Rider, 2008.

Vennard, Jane. *Praying with Body and Soul: A Way to Intimacy with God*. Minneapolis: Augsburg, 1998.

Ware, Kallistos. *The Power of the Name*. Oxford: SLG Press, 1974.

Webb, Chris. *The Fire of the Word: Meeting God on Holy Ground*. Downers Grove, Illinois: IVP Books USA, 2011.

Weil, Simone. *Gravity and Grace*. London: Routledge, 2002.

Weisheipl, James A. *Friar Thomas D'Aquino: His Life, Thought and Work*. New York: Doubleday, 1974.

Wuellner, Flora Slosson. *Prayer, Stress, and Our Inner Wounds*. Nashville: The Upper Room, 1985.

Printed in Great Britain
by Amazon